The Christ
of the Mount

The Christ of the Mount

A Working Philosophy of Life

E. Stanley Jones

ABINGDON

Nashville

THE CHRIST OF THE MOUNT

A Festival Book

Festival edition published March 1981

ISBN 0-687-06925-4

CONTENTS

DIVIDED PERSONALITY THE REASON WE DO NOT ATTAIN THE GOAL

THE WAY OUT

PREFACE

FOR the last two years about twenty-five selected men and women, Indian and foreign, have met in the Sat Tal Ashram for two and a half months during the summer for quiet prayer and serious thinking in regard to our Christian message. There in that secluded Himalayan retreat we faced life and God. We opened our minds to the best in other faiths and studied them seriously. And then we asked ourselves whether in Christ we had a message that was vital and inescapable if we were to find life and God.

In thinking of the moral implications of the gospel we were driven at once to the Sermon on the Mount. Was it a valid and vital and practical way to live?

The first year the writer led the group through the Sermon and discussed it with them. He placed before them the general views contained in this book. During the following year this book was written. This year he had the privilege of placing the completed manuscript before the group and of discussing it with them for an hour a day for about twenty days. He received many valuable criticisms and suggestions, and gratefully acknowledges the indebtedness he owes to this group. But he cannot hold them responsible for the views presented here. The responsibility rests upon the writer.

While acknowledging the above indebtedness, there is at the same time the consciousness of the deeper debt he owes to the Divine Companion, "the Spirit of Truth." He hopes and trusts that something of his Mind has been worked into these pages. But the word "something" is all that he dare use—the rest belongs to Him. Let the reader find that "something" in these pages and live by it—and forget the rest.

E. STANLEY JONES.

Sitapur, U. P. India.

INTRODUCTION

MEN need nothing in these modern days so much as they need a working philosophy of life—an adequate way to live. "The real concern and confusion of this age," as Lord Haldane said, "is not so much religious, or even intellectual, as moral." Loosed from the moorings that have held life many are now adrift. They claim to be free. They have thrown overboard the chart, the compass, the steering wheel, and the consciousness of destination. They are free from everything—everything except the rocks, and the storms, and the insufferable inanity of being tossed from wave to wave of mere meaningless emotion.

The modern man is "left by science without a goal; by exploded humanitarianism without a hero; by logic with an impasse"—he needs a way out. Can religion provide it? Certainly, irreligion does not seem to have found the way to live. Take Nietzsche. He raved against the way of Jesus as "slave morality." He would be free. Was he? He cried: "Where is my home? For it do I ask and have sought, but have not found it. O eternal everywhere, O eternal nowhere, O eternal in vain." The sting is in the last two words, "in vain." The sense of futility, of meaningless striving, has settled upon many. It is so in the West, it is so in the East.

"I have no solution to the problem of life and of suffering and I seem to be predestined to have no solution," said an earnest Hindu in one of our Round Table Conferences. Said another, a Hindu professor: "I began to give up one thing after another and then I found that everything was gone, even my universe. I was also ready to give up myself and commit suicide. My life is getting duller and duller every day. It has no meaning. But maybe there will something work out of it. So far it has brought me *nil*." A chairman of a meeting in which I had spoken on a working philosophy of life said: "I have lived a long time, but as yet I have no philosophy of life, let alone a working philosophy of life. I am inwardly a chaos, full of clash and confusion, and I dare say that there are many of you here who are like me." There *are* many who are like him—increasingly so. Nor are they all outside of the Christian Church. The Christian is asking with increasing anxiety, and I believe with increasing sincerity, "What is the Christian's working way to live?"

A brilliant lady in high society in the West, who had stumbled on the treasure hid in the field of human life, and had gone off and for joy thereof had sold all that she had to buy that field, said to the writer: "Now that I am a Christian what are you going to do with me? How does one act as a Christian? What is the technique of being a Christian?"

I did not answer this penetrating question at once, because—well, I wasn't sure, and the sincerity of the question demanded that I be sure. Now, after months and years of brooding amid the storm and clash of things, I have come to the conclusion that what we call the Sermon on the Mount is the way a Christian will act, that it constitutes the technique of being a Christian— it is his working philosophy of life.

Among the many things which India has taught me are two outstanding: first, she compelled me to disentangle Christ from the accretions which the centuries had gathered around him. It was a liberating experience to find one's faith becoming simplified and centered in a Person. For years I have walked in that liberty; but for several years there has been an undertone of questioning, and rather troubled questioning. The question was this: Yes, Christ is the center, and to be a Christian is to catch his mind and his spirit, but what main content should be in those words—"Christ," "Christian"? It is not enough to have the words. The deeper question concerns the content that is to be in the words. For the content varies, and varies vitally. So India has taught me the second thing: the main moral content in the word "Christian" must be the Sermon on the Mount.

India is forcing us to face anew the Sermon

on the Mount. She insists that this is Christianity. No matter how much we may point to our creeds she insists on pointing us to the pattern shown her in the Mount. The fact is that the Sermon on the Mount is not in our creeds. As the Apostles' Creed now stands you can accept every word of it and leave the essential self untouched. Suppose we had written it in our creeds and had repeated each time with conviction: "I believe in the Sermon on the Mount and in its way of life, and I intend, God helping me, to embody it"! What would have happened? I feel sure that if this had been our main emphasis, the history of Christendom would have been different. With emphasis on doctrines which left unaffected our way of life the Christian Church could accept Constantine as its prize convert. And yet Constantine, after his alleged conversion, murdered his conquered colleague and brother-in-law Licinius; sentenced to death his eleven-year-old nephew, killed his eldest son, Crispus; brought about the death of his second wife; took the nails that were supposed to come from the cross of Christ and used one in his war helmet and another on the bridle of his war horse. Yet he was canonized by the Greek Church and his memory celebrated "as equal to the apostles." He talked and presided at the opening of the Council of Nicæa, which was called to frame a creed, and he was hailed as "a bishop of bishops." Could this have happened if the men who had gathered there had made the Sermon on the Mount an essential part of the Creed? It had no place in it, so Constantine could be at home. What had happened was that the Christian Church had been conquered by a pagan warrior. And the church allowed itself to be thus conquered, for this ideal of Christ did not have possession of its soul. For the same reason, a bishop could kick another to death in the cathedral of Constantinople to prove his orthodoxy, and the Monophysites of Alexander could cry, "As thou hast divided, so shalt thou be divided," and then proceed to butcher those who believed in the dual nature of Christ in order to prove that the nature of Christ was one and indivisible.

These things sound strange to our ears, but it is only because the ideas of the Sermon on the Mount are reasserting their ascendency over our spirit and are beginning to come back as central in the thinking of the Christian. Even now it is far from being an essential part of our Christian thinking. Even now, in many quarters, the orthodoxy of the creed is looked on as more essential than the orthopraxy of the deed. We have saluted this ideal, but have not taken it seriously. We have used it for polemic, but not for practice. We have done as the British officers did in one of the battles of the Sikh war: they shut up the commanding general in a high tower, locked the door, and then went out and fought the battle on their own principles. We have locked this ideal of Christ in high towers of reverence and respect and have then gone off to fight the battle of life in our own way, on our own principles, or lack of them—to our disaster.

The greatest need of modern Christianity is the rediscovery of the Sermon on the Mount as the only practical way to live. Now we have an undertone of doubt and fear that it is not workable. We feel that it is trying to give human nature a bent that it will not take; it is trying to force something on us for which human nature is not made. Housman puts it in these lines:

"And since, my soul, we cannot flee
    To Saturn or to Mercury,
    Keep we must, if keep we can,
    Those foreign laws of God and man."

Are the principles laid down in the Sermon on the Mount foreign laws? Are they something for which we are not made? It would seem so —at first sight. Chesterton says that on the first reading you feel that it turns everything upside down, but the second time you read it you discover that it turns everything right side up. The first time you read it you feel that it is impossible, the second time, you feel that nothing else is possible. The more I have pondered on this way of life, the more I am persuaded that instead of all the moral impossibilities lying in the Sermon on the Mount, as we often think, the fact is that all the moral possibilities lie here, and all the impossibilities lie outside.

We have become so naturalized in other ways of life that this way seems foreign. I sat for a long time with my legs twisted under me and when I got up to walk it was exceedingly painful to straighten them out and difficult to move along. I had sat in an unnatural position so long that the natural functioning of the legs seemed unnatural. But only for a few moments! A wolf-child, captured near where I live in India, had lived with wolves from the age of two to the age of eleven. It ran on all-fours. Its knee-joints were stiff and enlarged from running in this fashion. It would eat only raw meat, and when it was put on a more civilized diet, it took dysentery and died. A human being had lived in a wolf environment on wolf principles, on a wolf diet for nine years. Human nature had so accommodated itself to it that it seemed the natural way to live and our more human ways seemed unnatural. We have lived so long on the wolf-principles of selfishness and competition and strife that the Christian way of unselfishness, of co-operation, and love seems to us a foreign way.

The Sermon on the Mount may seem impossible, but only in our worst moments. In our highest moments—that is, in our real moments —we feel that everything else is unbelievably impossible, an absurdity. When we get this insight, we are inwardly conscious that it is foresight.

But nowhere has the gospel been more emasculated and explained away than here. One commentator of modern days says that "we must not degrade these words by a grotesque literalism." No, nor must we denature them by an ingratiating and inane spiritualizing. The danger is not literalism, but literaryism—explaining away its stark challenge by literary devices. Years ago when I asked Mahatma Gandhi what we could do to naturalize Christianity in India so that it would cease to be a foreign thing, among other things he replied: "Practice your religion without adulterating it or toning it down"—and he had in mind the Sermon on the Mount. It is Mahatma Gandhi's literal insistence upon this way of acting in gaining political freedom that has startled and challenged the whole Western world. He has proved that it is possible, and that is power. This fresh discovery, by a Hindu, of a truth long buried beneath the armaments of the fighting West has been one of the most important spiritual discoveries of modern times. When I wrote to a discerning friend in the West that I was preparing to write a book on this subject, he replied, "I suppose you just had to write this book." He was right. I did. With this challenge facing us, of a non-Christian nation acting, on a widespread scale, on one of the most profound principles of the Sermon on the Mount we have now no alternative but to be Christian according to this pattern, or cease to be Christians in any effective sense at all. We must now cease to embalm it. We must embody it—or abdicate.

A Moslem college professor arose at the close of one of my meetings and thanked me for saying what I had been saying, but urged me that I go to the West and preach this Sermon on the Mount to them, that they needed it. The applause that greeted his statement showed that the audience agreed. I replied that I would, but that human need and human sin were not geographical, that in a round world it is difficult to tell where East begins and West ends, that we are all in the same deep need. While I believed my answer was true, nevertheless concerning the Sermon on the Mount there are just two great questions, one from the East and one from the West. The East asks, *"Will* you work it?" And the West, *"Can* we work it?" Is it workable? The crux of the religious problem of the world is just here. Dean Inge rightly says that if Christianity cannot hold us at the place of ethical conduct, if it loses the battle at that place, then what is left is not worth fighting over. For mind you, if the ethical side of our gospel is unworkable, then by that very fact the redemptive side is rendered worthless. The center and substance of the Christian's ethical conduct is in the Sermon on the Mount. If this is unworkable, then there is not much left. We must turn our conduct over to other ways of living and stand beside dead altars, repeating dead creeds.

We have insisted that what we call Christian experience is an absolute necessity and that without that which Pentecost provides we cannot be Christian in any vital sense. This is true. But it must be remembered that back of Pentecost lay the Sermon on the Mount. When the disciples received the divine re-enforcement, it ran into these channels of conduct. Pentecost had the content of the Sermon on the Mount in it and therefore the power manifested was Christian. Pentecost divorced from the Sermon on the Mount is spiritual pow-wow instead of spiritual power.

But this way of life has been toned down and made "safe." The Marquis of Wellesley, a hundred years ago, said that it was "dangerous to send the Bible to India with its ideas of human equality without the safeguard of a commentary." The Marquis was right. The Bible, with its ideas of human equality, was dangerous to the kind of society that existed in India, organized as it was on caste. It was dangerous also to the kind of an empire that existed in Britain, organized as it was on the right of the white to rule. These ideas of human equality have been working since then and the result has been that a new democratic India is coming into being, and the empire has been changed and saved by its granting the right of self-rule to each constituent part, including India. What was looked on as a danger turned out to be a door.

The Sermon on the Mount seems dangerous. It challenges the whole underlying conception on which modern society is built. It would replace it by a new conception, animate it with a new motive, and turn it toward a new goal. One day I was addressing an audience of Hindus and Moslems and was interpreting the Sermon on the Mount. Before me sat two C. I. D. men, secret service police taking down shorthand notes of what I was saying, to be sent to the government to see if anything seditious could be found in it. A Christian government sends Hindu and Moslem agents to find out if the Sermon on the Mount is seditious! It is! The ideas underlying the Sermon on the Mount are the charter of freedom to all men, of all races, of all climes, of all classes. The secret police of the Modern Economic Order might have sent their agents to see if there is anything seditious against their Order in this Sermon. There is! This Sermon strikes at the whole selfish competitive idea underlying modern economic life and demands that men co-operate in love or perish in strife. The Militarists might have sent their secret police to see if there was anything seditious against their methods in the Sermon. There is! The Sermon challenges the whole conception of force which militarism holds and would substitute the method of love. The churches might have sent representatives to see if there is anything seditious against them. There is! Denominationalism often expresses itself in ways that are not much more than an ecclesiastical race in competitive armaments. It would find the Sermon on the Mount seditious, for it demands that individuals and groups and nations lose themselves in co-operation that they may find themselves in a higher brotherhood.

The Sermon on the Mount was and is seditious. It finally put Jesus on the cross, and it will do the same for his followers who follow it in modern life. But it would not end there. There would be a resurrection so great, so transforming in human living that we would know by actual experimentation that it is the only way for us to live.

The little girl, of whom Doctor Glover tells, unwittingly expressed this challenging side of the gospel when she said to her sister, "Barbara, I tell you the Bible does *not* end in Timothy; it ends in Revolutions." It does! The mother of Jesus caught this note in the gospel when, as she saw what would happen with the impact of Jesus upon life, she broke out in inspired song: "He hath scattered the proud in the imagination of their heart" (a personal revolution). "He hath put down princes from their thrones" (practical revolution), "and hath exalted them of low degree" (social revolution). "The hungry he hath filled with good things and the rich he hath sent empty away" (economic revolution). Here was the Great Change introduced into life. It would go through the whole of life from the personal to the economic, the social and the political.

"One reason why we come to hear you," said an ardent Hindu nationalist one day, "is that while you say nothing about politics as such, yet you supply ideas from your gospel upon which the movements for freedom in India can live." The Sermon on the Mount is the original charter of human freedom. A Hindu nationalist stood before the court and said to the Christian public prosecutor: "We have learned from your Bible our ideas of freedom. We are teaching them to our people, and for that you put us into jail." Someone has said that "it is now impossible in the English language to argue a man into slavery." The ideas of freedom have so permeated the language that it can no longer be used as a vehicle to bind men in slavery. Let anyone be saturated with the thought of the Sermon on the Mount and he will not only not try to argue a man into slavery, but he will not rest till every man is free, including himself.

"We love the Christ of the Sermon on the Mount and the Christ of the Seamless Robe at Calvary, but the Christ of dogmatism—No!" said a thoughtful Hindu to me one day. Are they different? Have the Christ of the Sermon on the Mount and the Christ of the creeds become different? If so, then the greatest task before Christendom is to bring them together. For no other kind of Christianity can lead this turbulent age.

A little man in a loin cloth in India picks out from the Sermon on the Mount one of its central principles, applies it as a method for gaining human freedom, and the world, challenged and charmed, bends over to catch the significance of the great sight. It is a portent of what would happen if we would take the whole of the Sermon on the Mount and apply it to the whole of life. It would renew our Christianity—it would renew the world. Our present-day Christianity, anæmic and weak from the parasites that have fastened themselves on its life through the centuries, needs a blood-transfusion from the Sermon on the Mount in order to renew radiant health within it that it may throw off these parasites and arise to serve and save the world.

But will this ideal work? Is it practicable? Just here is the central area of our skepticism. We are not quite sure that the Sermon on the Mount is the Sermon for the mart. We are not sure, and an unsure place is an unsafe place. We must go on or go back. We must be more Christian or less.

I trust this book will be an unhesitating, but not a too-light, easy, "Yes" to the question as to whether the Sermon on the Mount is practicable. If the reading of it brings to the reader what the writing of it has brought to the writer in these months of meditation, then we will both be repaid a hundredfold. A trusted friend said to the writer, "You are not a theologian; you are a divining rod. You tell us where there is water beneath—remember your function." In this book I have tried to remember my function. I have left to others the discussion of the critical questions involved in the accounts of the Sermon on the Mount as reported by Matthew and Luke. I have not been able to escape theological implications—who can escape them?— but I have tried to leave to the theologians the labeling of the wells and their more accurate description while I have endeavored to be true to my friend's commission and have pointed to where in the Sermon on the Mount I think water may be found. There *is* water here—dig and drink!

PERFECTION EXEMPLIFIED AND DEFINED

CHAPTER I

THE MAN ON THE MOUNT

WE call this the Sermon on the Mount. In doing so we do it an injustice and lower its tone. In a sermon we take a text and expound it. There is nothing of that here. This is not a sermon—it is a portrait, a portrait of Jesus himself, and of the Father and of the man-to-be. True, he does not set out to present a portrait of himself, but as he draws the lines in the picture of the Father and of the man-to-be we find he is dipping his brush into the deeps of his own life and experience, and gradually we see that "one dear Face," the interpretation of both God and man. We have here not the lines of a code but the lineaments of a Character.

Jesus is the simplification of God.' All great discoveries are simplifications. Thought moves from the complicated to the simple. "The curious fact remains," says Professor Vaughan, "that in science and in philosophy the cumbersome, interminable hypothesis comes first, especially to a type of the learned mind; the simple and adequate hypothesis appears last." All the great philosophical and religious systems of Greece and India and China were completed and reached their height just before the time of the

27

coming of Christ. One is deeply impressed with the mental acumen of the men who wrote the Upanishads, but he is also deeply impressed by the complications, the intricacies, and the mazes of their thought about God. They suffer from mental overstrain. Men will probably never again go so far in the complicated use of words in the setting forth of the Divine as did these writers in the Sanskrit. They were ultimates in words. What was needed was the ultimate Word. Then the Great Simplification took place. The Word became flesh.

Jesus is called the Word because the word is the expression of the hidden thought. Unless I put my thought into words you cannot understand it. Here is God; we sense his presence, but he is Spirit, hence hidden. We want to know what he is like—not in omnipotence, nor in omniscience, nor in omnipresence; a revelation of these would do little or no good, but we would know his character, for what he is like in character, we, his children, must be. So the Hidden Thought—God—becomes the Revealed Word—Christ.

My words are the incarnation of, the offspring of, the son of my thought. So the Word, Jesus, is the Son of the Thought, God. As we look up through the words of a man to understand his thought, so we look up through Jesus to know what God is like. He is like that which we see in Jesus. And if he is, then he is a good God and trustable. I can ask nothing better. Streeter puts it in this way: "Suppose your child would come to you and ask, 'Is God as wise as Einstein?' You would probably laugh. But if the child should say, 'Is God as good as Jesus?' you should be able to say that God is better than any man, but in your heart of hearts you would probably say (to yourself and not to the child) that the real question is, Is God as good as Jesus?" This is not overdrawn, for the modern doubt is not concerning Jesus, but concerning God. "I do not understand God, but the character of Jesus is the one thing that holds my universe steady," said a brilliant man in our Round Table Conferences. A doctor from Europe protested when I wrote this sentence: "If the Heart that is back of the universe is like this gentle heart that broke upon the cross, he can have my heart without qualification," saying, "I agree with you when you say that life lived according to Jesus is the best and finest that we know, but why do you write the word 'heart' with a capital 'H,' as if the horrible being back of the universe had a heart?" This doctor's doubt was not concerning Jesus but concerning God. But Jesus said and showed that they were one—"I and my Father are one." Just as the word and the thought are one, so Jesus and the Father are one.

In another place Jesus said, "The Father is greater than I." Are these not contradictory? No, not necessarily, for while the thought and the word are one, nevertheless the thought is greater than the word. All expression of thought by words means the limitation of thought. You have to look around to see if you can find the word that will adequately express the thought. So God, expressed in the Word, is limited by the very nature of the case. The Father —the unexpressed God, is greater than the Son —the expressed God. And yet they are one.

A man's words are, for those outside him, the way to his thought. So Jesus, the Word, is the way to the Thought, God. But my words are not a third something standing between you and my thought; they are my thought projected to you, my thought become available. If you take hold of my words, you take hold of my very thought. Jesus is not a Third Person standing between me and God. Rather he is God projected to me, God become available. He is a mediator in the sense that he mediates God to me, for when I take hold of him I take hold of the very self of God.

This Word is not a spelled-out Word, it is a lived-out Word. He is indeed the speech of eternity translated into the language of time, but the language is a Life. God's method is a Man. Jesus is God speaking to the man in the street. He is God meeting me in my environment, a human environment. He is God showing his character in the place where our characters are formed. He is the human life of God. He is that part of God which we have been able to see. And if the rest of God is like this that we have been able to see, then all is right. God means well and he means to make us well.

But the Life was truly human. He met life as a man. He called on no power for his own moral battle that is not at your disposal and mine. He did perform miracles, but only for others and in answer to human need. He performed no miracles for himself. His character was an achievement. Everything he laid before men in the words spoken on the Mount had gone through his own soul. They were livable, for he was living them. "We are glad to read about the Man who practiced everything he preached," wrote some Hindu students to whom Bibles were presented on their graduation. He did.

The Sermon on the Mount is practicable, for the Man who first spoke these words practiced them, and the practicing of them produced a character so beautiful, so symmetrical, so compelling, so just what life ought to be, that he is as inescapable in the moral realm as the force of gravity is in the physical.

The words of the Sermon must be interpreted in the light of that Face. He puts a new content into old words by the illustration of his own life. In interpreting the Sermon on the Mount we have often applied methods of historical criticism and have taken words to mean what they meant in an Old Testament or in a contemporaneous setting. We may gain much for this

method, but we may also entirely miss the point
and reduce the whole to an echo of scattered sayings out of the past. His hearers did not feel
that way about it, for they were struck with the
utter newness of what he was saying: They
"were astonished at his teaching: for he taught
them as one having authority, and not as their
scribes."

You may point to parallel sayings in the past,
and yet when you do, you miss the central thing
here, for the central thing was the aroma about
the words, the contagion of his moral Person, the
sense of depth that came from the fact that he
spoke them—and illustrated them. He was not
presenting a new set of laws, but demanding a
new loyalty to his person. The loyalty to his
person was to be expressed in carrying out the
things he embodied. He was the embodiment of
the Sermon on the Mount, and to be loyal to
him meant to be loyal to his way of life. "For
righteousness sake" was the word of the past;
"for my sake" was the new word. "For righteousness sake" was the fulfillment of a law; "for
my sake" was the fulfillment of a Life. The
astonishing thing is that he uses them both and
makes them synonymous (Matthew 5. 10, 11),
and thereby claims incidentally that he was the
embodiment of the righteousness of the universe.
The new law was a Life. This lifted goodness
out of legalism and based it on love.

The essential difference between Pharisaism

and the teaching of Jesus is just here: "One was devotion to an idea—the Law; the other was devotion to a Person—the Gospel." In the first, one could feel that he had attained and could stand in the temple and thank God that he was not as other men; but the other could never feel that he had attained, for love was always opening new doors. The one produced the perfect Pharisee and the other the perfect lover. "If religion is concerned with love to a person there can be no limit to duty and there can be no question of merit," says Findlay, and he laid his finger upon an essential truth. There is a beyondness in the Sermon on the Mount that startles and appalls the legalistic mind. It sees no limit to duty—the first mile does not suffice, he will go two; the coat is not enough, he will give the cloak also; to love friends is not enough, he will love enemies as well. Come to that with the legalistic mind and it is impossible and absurd; come to it with the mind of the lover and nothing else is possible. The lover's attitude is not one of duty, but one of privilege. Here is the key to the Sermon on the Mount. We mistake it entirely if we look on it as the chart of the Christian's duty, rather it is the charter of the Christian's liberty—his liberty to go beyond, to do the thing that love impels and not merely the thing that duty compels. The fact is that this is not a law at all, but a lyre which we strike with the fingers of love in glad devotion. This glad, gay piety is the expression of a love from within and not the compression of a dull law from without.

Put the Man who spoke these words into the background and look only at the sayings and they become as lofty as Himalayan peaks—and as impossible. But put the warm touch of his reinvigorating fellowship into it, and anything —everything becomes possible, for these things were not to be worked out on the unit principle, but on the co-operative plan.

I said above that Jesus was the great simplification of God. He is also the simplification of duty. "Love and do what you like," he says in essence. And the things you will like will be just these "impossible" things which he lays down here in the Sermon.

But he is not only the simplification of God and of duty, he is also the simplification of words. Never were words reduced to their inmost essence as here. They are so reduced that they seem to cease to function as words and become facts. Of someone it was said that "his words were half-battles." The words of Jesus were whole facts. Get hold of these words and you will find that you have hold of the Word. The Sermon on the Mount is the Man on the Mount.

But this Word is an unfolding Word. "I have yet many things to say unto you, but ye cannot bear them now." He is saying things to each generation as they are able to hear and respond. We have not fully interpreted the Interpreter. In New Testament days it was said that when the people heard Him, "they were beyond measure astonished, saying, He hath done all things well; he maketh even the deaf to hear, and the dumb to speak." Yes, thank God, he hath done all things well, but this interpretation is too narrow. "All things well" means far more than making the deaf to hear and the dumb to speak. We now see that "all things well" means that he set before us a perfect ideal of human living, gave us a philosophy of life, met sin, suffering, and death at the cross, arose and redeems and leads the ages and throws open the gates of full life to all men. Perhaps the ages to come will say that we have been trying to interpret him in a too narrow and small a way.

This book does not come with any air of finality in the interpretation of these words of Jesus. Its purpose will be accomplished if it enlarges our view of the enlarging Christ. For he is God's final but unfolding Word.

CHAPTER II

THE GOAL OF HUMAN LIVING

MOST of us look on the Sermon on the Mount as a series of disconnected, or at the best very loosely connected, ethical exhortations. This, it seems to me, misses its point and its purpose. It has a center, and the entire Sermon revolves about that center, so that it is a co-ordinated whole. The center is the astonishing statement, "Be ye therefore perfect, even as your Father which is in heaven is perfect." Around this as the central ideal the Sermon revolves as on a pivot.

The Sermon naturally falls into six great divisions:

I. The goal of life: To be perfect or complete as the Father in heaven is perfect or complete (chapter 5, verse 48).

(a) The twenty-seven marks of this perfect life (chapter 5, verses 1-47).

II. A diagnosis of the reason why men do not reach or move on to that goal: Divided personality (chapters 6 and 7, verses 1-6).

III. The Divine offer of an adequate moral and spiritual re-enforcement so that men can move on to that goal: The Holy Spirit to them that ask him (chapter 7, verses 7-11).

IV. After making the Divine offer he gathers

up and emphasizes in two sentences our part in reaching that goal. Toward others—we are to do unto others as we would that they should do to us (chapter 7, verse 12); toward ourselves— we are to lose ourselves by entering the straight gate (chapter 7, verse 13).

V. The test of whether we are moving on to that goal, or whether this Divine Life is operative within us: By their fruits (chapter 7, verses 15-23).

VI. The survival value of this new life and the lack of survival value of life lived in any other way: The house founded on rock and the house founded on sand (chapter 7, verses 24-27).

We need, and need desperately, a redefining of what the goal of life is to be. If we are to have an adequate philosophy of life, we must be sure about what we are striving for ultimately. We must see the goal if we are to tread the way to it with any degree of confidence. But the goal of life in Christendom is very hazy and uncertain. It is usually taken for granted that the goal is to reach heaven. Our hymns express our deepest longings. Read through them and note the proportion of them that end up in the last verse with some note about heaven. A Hindu government official of high standing remarked before a highly intelligent audience: "Now the Hindus after working out their destiny through many rebirths have as their final goal union with the Divine. You Christians after this life have heaven granted to you as a reward for following Christ. Please enlarge on this." I found myself inwardly squirming at his statement of what he took for granted was the Christian goal. It seems cheap and morally tawdry to put our goal of life as heaven, given in reward for faithful service, alongside the majestic system of karma, in which a man works out his destiny through countless rebirths as the result of what he has done and been.

But squirm as we may, and explain away as we can, it is true nevertheless that a granted heaven and an imposed hell hold the field in the mind of Christendom as the final goal. I do not mean to assert that all of Christendom holds this view, but I do believe that in the minds of the majority this view does hold the field. I say "in the mind of Christendom," for when I turn to the New Testament to find out what its goal is, I see something else. Its goal is that man is to be perfect as the Father in heaven is perfect. This is not an isolated statement contained in the Sermon on the Mount. It is the theme of the New Testament.

Apart from the book of Revelation, which we leave aside for a moment, the New Testament speaks in thirty-three places of perfection as the goal. It mentions heaven about twelve times as a place to which men will go hereafter. I do not mean to include in this "the kingdom of heaven" which, of course, must not be identified with heaven as a place, since in one of its phases, at least, it is "within you." But in not one of the twelve places is it said that heaven is the goal of life. Heaven is set down as the framework of something more important at the center, that central thing is perfection of character as the Father in heaven is perfect. Heaven is a by-product of perfected being. Turn to these thirty-three places where perfection is mentioned and you will find that it is not marginal and incidental, but central and emphatic. Take several: "And he gave some, apostles; and some, prophets; and some, evangelists; and some, pastors and teachers: for the perfecting of the saints, for the work of the ministry, for the edifying of the body of Christ: till we all come in the unity of the faith, and of the knowledge of the Son of God, unto a perfect man, unto the measure of the stature of the fullness of Christ" (Ephesians 4. 11-13). Here the end of the work of the apostle, the prophet, the evangelist, the pastor and the teacher is to produce a perfect man—perfect, after no mean pattern, but according to the measure of the stature of the fullness of Christ. In the Sermon on the Mount we are to be perfect as the Father is perfect and here we are to be perfect according to the stature of Christ, but as they are one the goal is one. Jesus in another place put the goal in these words: "But every one that is perfected shall be as his master" (Luke 6. 40).

Paul says again: "Not as though I had already attained, either were already perfect; but I follow after, if that I may apprehend that for which I am apprehended of Christ Jesus. . . . I press toward the mark for the prize of the high calling of God in Christ Jesus" (Philippians 3. 12-14). What was the prize? The prize evidently was that he be "perfect," and it was for nothing less than this that he was "apprehended" or laid hold of by Christ. Again: "Whom we preach, warning every man, and teaching every man in all wisdom; that we may present every man perfect in Christ: whereunto I also labor" (Colossians 1. 28, 29). The end of Paul's labor was not that his converts should attain heaven, but that every man might be perfect. When Jesus said to the rich young ruler, "If thou wouldest be perfect, go, sell that thou hast," he did not mean that the selling of all would make him perfect, but that it would clear away the hindrances and would put his feet on the pathway to perfection.

The ideal of the perfection of the human personality held the field in the New Testament until the book of Revelation was written. It was written out of a period of persecution and Christians saw heaven as release. Since then the emphasis has been shifted and heaven and hell now hold the field. It is cheaper and easier. I do not mean that in the book of Revelation there is not the note of the redemption of moral char-

acter. There is. But men found it easier to
take the framework of an outer heaven which is
there depicted than the fact of an inner perfection of character which is the center of that
heaven. The New Testament emphasis must be
restored. For if the goal of the Christian is to
be nothing less than the perfection of the individual in moral and spiritual character then I
can straighten my shoulders and look the world
of thoughtful people squarely in the eye, for this
goal is not morally cheap or easy or tawdry. It
is a goal that I can morally respect with all my
heart. I know nothing finer.

Moreover, this goal of life is in line with the
development going on through nature which
seems, in the words of Tagore, "to lift up strong
hands toward perfection."

But the word "perfection" makes us shy a bit.
It seems too finished and closed. Perhaps the
conception of "the complete life" would make us
less hesitant than the perfect life. But to get
the New Testament conception we must mean
complete—plus.

The final goal of each of the systems might be
stated as follows:

Hebrews: Ye therefore shall dwell in the house
of the Lord forever, even as Jehovah your God
will reward you.

Hinduism: Ye therefore shall be merged into
the Impersonal, even into Brahma, the Impersonal.

Buddhism: Ye therefore shall dwell on the borderland of being and not-being, even as Nirvana is being and not-being.

Islam: Ye therefore shall have a paradise of pleasure, even as Allah, the Almighty wills.

The Greeks: Ye therefore shall dwell with the gods and be happy, even as the gods are brightly and sensuously happy.

Humanism: Ye therefore shall cease to be, even as all things shall end in dissolution.

Christ: Ye therefore shall be perfect as the Father in heaven is perfect.

This goal that Christ sets before us is one concerning which we need not apologize. It says to the humanist that it goes beyond humanism in its affirmation of human values. It affirms man even unto perfection. It makes humanism with its small views of man's final destiny seem inhumanism. It puts worth and dignity and meaning into human personality. A complete God and a complete man are to be in the same universe. Its goal is not a negation but a mighty affirmation. "Ye," the essential *you* will be perfect. The East is not only world-weary, it is personality-weary. Its endeavor is not only to get rid of the world, but also to get rid of personality whether in Nirvana or in Brahma. Therefore the world is nothing and moral values have no final meaning—they belong to the state that will be sloughed off in the final release. But the gospel is world-affirming and morality-affirming because it is personality-affirming. Jesus says: "Whosoever will save his life shall lose it; but whosoever shall lose his life for my sake . . . shall save it," or "save it alive," as some translate it. The personality is finally affirmed, it is "saved alive." Buddhism saves it dead. Hinduism saves it by losing its identity in God. The gospel alone saves it alive.

Moreover, if we are to be perfect as the Father in heaven is perfect, then the same moral laws that govern God's acting must govern ours. In other words, the moral laws are not rooted in the shifting customs of men, but they are rooted in the very nature of the Divine. This gives us a stable moral universe and it means that moral distinctions have ultimate meaning. Moral laws are not based on the divine will, but on the divine nature. They are not whimsical, for God is not whimsical. They are dependable and orderly, for God is dependable and orderly. I can morally respect a God who will act on everything he requires of man. The universe is then all of a piece—it is a universe and not a multiverse.

"By all that God requires of me,
I know that he himself must be."

Here is an essential difference between the gospel and other ways of life; Hinduism and Buddhism base their ethics on the law of karma, which is independent of God; Islam bases its morality on the will of God; Christ bases it on the nature and being of God. These moral laws are the very expression of his being and he asks of man nothing that he himself does not practice. Emerson puts it in these words:

"Not mine to look where cherubim and seraphs may not see.
But nothing can be good in him which evil is in me."

A thoughtful Hindu editor summed it up for me in this way: "Hinduism is God without morality; Buddhism is morality without God; Christianity is God with morality."

It has been suggested that the Sermon on the Mount has come from Buddhist sources, but this overlooks the essential difference between the two conceptions of morality—one bases it on the impersonal law of karma, which takes no cognizance of God whatever, and the other bases it on the very nature and being of God. Moreover, in the one personality is finally lost and in the other it is finally affirmed and perfected as God is perfect. The differences are wider than the agreements.

Many who have taught Christian perfection, as Wesley, in order to bring perfection within the borders of this life have taught that the perfection spoken of in the Sermon on the Mount is perfection only in love and not in character and conduct. Certainly, the perfection spoken of here includes perfection in love as its beginning and basis and this can be found within the borders of this life; but if that is all, then the perfection is not perfect enough, for perfection in love is often claimed along with very great imperfection in character and conduct. No, the perfection mentioned here is more far-reaching than that—we are to be perfect as the Father in heaven is perfect, not, of course, in infinitude and quantity, but certainly in quality. This visualizes something which, while it begins in this life, cannot be confined to or be completed within the boundaries of this life, but throws open the possibility of ages of growth and development. A heaven in which ages of growth in perfection would be before us would be a heaven worth while.

If perfection and not pleasure be the goal, then this universe had to be a universe of discipline, of pain, and even of hardness. I need this kind of a school if my graduation means *that*. "Genius is developed in solitude, but character is made in the stream of life" amid buffetings and blessings. I accept the curriculum of this school, for I want its possible outcome—character. One of the greatest needs of modern religious life in Christendom is discipline. It has been, on the whole, too cheap and easy. The goal of perfection would put this much-needed discipline into Christian life.

Be ye therefore perfect as the Father in heaven is perfect—what a goal for human life! What depth and dignity and meaning it puts into life!

"I am the tadpole of an archangel," cried some-one. But I am more: I am the embryo of the man who is to be perfect as the Father is perfect. Then let nothing stop me. I cannot tarry by the wayside. O littleness, lay no cramping hand on me, for I am made for the great; O flesh, do not ensnare me, for I am out for high destiny; O world, teach me, but do not entangle me, for the perfect calls me. And I must go.

THE NEW TYPE OF HUMANITY

CHAPTER III

WHAT THEY ARE IN THEMSELVES

At first thought, perfection as the goal of life seems too individualistic and too other-worldly —the two deadly theological sins, according to modern men. Taken out of its context this is true; in its context it is not true.

Jesus was addressing a group. While the "ye" in the "Ye shall be perfect" refers to them as individuals it also refers to them as a group—a group that represented the new humanity. Both the new man and the new society were to be perfect. If Jesus had presented this ideal of perfection in the opening verses of the Sermon, it would have arisen before men as abruptly, as lofty, and as grand as Mount Everest—and as uninviting. Instead of that he gradually unfolded a type of life so beautiful and so compelling that when he came to the climax there was nothing else to say except, "Be ye therefore perfect, even as your Father which is in heaven is perfect." Anything less would have been an anti-climax.

In forty-five living verses (Matthew 5. 3-47) he poured into the goal of perfection such a warm, human and this-worldly content that the goal, when stated, though not bounded by this life, was yet firmly grounded in this life and was one that must be wrought out in human relationships. The key to the verse, "Be ye therefore perfect," is the word "therefore." It points back, not merely to the preceding verses as some have thought, but to the whole of what he had been saying. It gathers up and pours into verse forty-eight the whole of the forty-five preceding verses and makes these the content of the perfection. From these verses we find that there are twenty-seven marks of the perfect life, and these marks show how deeply social and yet how deeply individual the ideal is.

The perfect life consists in being poor in spirit, in mourning, in being meek, in hungering and thirsting after righteousness, in being merciful, pure in heart, in being a peacemaker, persecuted for righteousness sake and yet rejoicing and being exceeding glad, in being the salt of the earth, the light of the world, having a righteousness that exceeds, in being devoid of anger with the brother, using no contemptuous words, allowing no one to hold anything against one, having the spirit of quick agreement, no inward lustful thinking, relentless against anything that offends against the highest, right relations in the home life, truth in speech and attitude, turning the other cheek, giving the cloak also, going the second mile, giving to those who ask and from those who would borrow turning not away, loving even one's enemies, praying for those who persecute—thus you will be sons of your Father and you will be perfect as your Father in heaven is perfect.

There is not one of these twenty-seven marks of the perfect life that is irrelevant or trifling and not one that is not utterly essential to the perfect life. Jesus is not only wonderful in what he put in, but also in what he left out. Someone has suggested that practically everything that Jesus taught could be found in the Talmud. "Yes," was the reply, "and very much more besides." The Talmud held treasures amid much rubbish. But Jesus hits the essential and always the essential. His was the sifted mind. He was never misled by a subordinate issue, never took a bypath and never missed the point. This will come out, I trust, as we look more specifically at these twenty-seven marks.

The presentation of the perfect life by Jesus divides itself into five major portions:

1. What believers are in themselves—the Beatitudes (verses 2-12).

2. What they are to the world—salt, light (verses 13-16).

3. What they are to the past—they fulfill rather than destroy (verses 17-20).

4. What they are in intimate relationships with others (verses 21-47).

5. What they shall be—perfect as the Father is perfect (verse 48).

Jesus begins at what they are to be in them-

selves. He begins at the center. He insisted
that men could not live at the circumference unless they were alive at the center. The modern
attempt is to have quantity of life at the circumference regardless of quality of life at the center.
Jesus knew this would end in futility and cynicism and utter shallowness. When he would
make all things new, he would first of all lay
his hand upon the human heart. He knew that
"you cannot make the golden age out of leaden
instincts." He spoke of what they were to be
(verses 2-13) before he spoke of what they were
to do and not do (rest of Sermon). He begins
by saying, "Blessed are"—what you are in yourselves determines life for you. You are your
own heaven and you are your own hell. He
knew that "hell often breaks out within man by
spontaneous combustion," and that heaven is a
state of mind before it can be a place. He came,
therefore, not to get men into heaven but to get
heaven into men; not to get men out of hell but
to get hell out of men. If "conduct is three
fourths of life," then character is the whole of
it, for "character is destiny."

To describe the state of those who are right
within he uses a word that is crammed full of
meaning—"Blessed." The word is *makarios,*
a word which Aristotle used for divine blessed-
ness in contrast with human happiness. The
ordinary word for human happiness was *euda-
monia,* but he passed that by as weak. Since we

are to partake of the perfection that God has, so we are to partake of the joy that is divine. The first note of Buddha's teaching is Suffering; the first note that Jesus strikes is Joy. But this happiness is not dependent on happenings. Its sources are within. "Blessed *are*." So this note of joy is not a jazz note—cheap, easy, and surface. It sounds the depths before it reaches the heights.

But the word "blessed" is more than joyful; it means literally, "not subject to fate," "deathless." It depicts the kind of life that rises above the fated mechanism of earthly life into moral and spiritual freedom. So the two meanings taken together would give the meaning of blessed, that is, "to be deathless and happy."

The Beatitudes are nine in number and they break themselves up into three groups of three each. The first group starts with, "Blessed are the poor in spirit; for theirs is the kingdom of heaven." Many guesses have been made at the meaning of "poor in spirit," some choosing the Old Testament meaning of "a poor remnant looking for the redemption of Israel," some taking it to be synonymous with "humility," and some, as Tertullian, making it mean, "beggars in spirit." None of these, it seems to me, sound its depth. They are too tame. We would expect Jesus to sound a more thoroughgoing, radical note in the very beginning. He does. The word Luke uses for "poor" is *ani*—one poor by circumstances, but the word used here is *anav*—one poor by choice. The word, then, that would come nearest to expressing its meaning would be "renounced in spirit."

There are just two great philosophies of life. Nietzsche summed up the one when he said: "Assert yourself. Care for nothing except for yourself. The only vice is weakness, and the only virtue is strength. Be strong, be a superman. The world is yours if you can get it." Here is the cult of self-expression. It is Darwinism as a philosophy of life. The method of survival in lower nature is turned into the method of survival among men. In Nietzsche this cult of self-expression is ruthless. In others it is refined; but they all hold that the way to find life is to look after yourself, whether by ruthless self-assertion or by refined self-culture. Jesus stands as the utter opposite of that, and says that the way to find life is to lose it, that the way of self-realization is by the way of self-renunciation. He says, "If any man would come after me, let him deny himself [literally, "utterly reject himself"], and take up his cross and follow me." No two ways could be more opposed. Nietzsche died in a madhouse and the world that followed him went to the brink of hell in the last war—a natural outcome of this self-assertive attitude. Its genesis is selfishness, its exodus is suicide.

Jesus strikes a blow at the self-assertive attitude in the very beginning. He says that this "self" must be renounced. In Mark 9. 43, he says, "It is better to enter into life maimed," and in verse 47: "It is better for thee to enter into the kingdom of God with one eye." Here "life" and "the kingdom of God" are used synonymously. This first beatitude could then read, "Deathless and happy are the renounced in spirit for theirs is life." They have found life—found it by letting it go. This is another way of putting that verse which, to me, is the center of Christ's teaching: "He that saveth his life shall lose it and he that loseth his life shall find it."

It is very interesting to note that Walter Lippmann, in his *Preface to Morals,* after letting God go, with somewhat of a pang, and turning wistfully to humanism, gives what he calls "a high religion." His high religion is this: "Learning not to demand anything of life that life does not contain; of limiting one's desires until they harmonize with reality; of facing life in the spirit of disinterestedness." . . . "We yearn for comfort, for success, for eternal life. High religion is regeneration from these desires." It is very remarkable that Hinduism, Buddhism, Lippmann, and Jesus all converge on one thing, namely, renunciation of desire. Lippmann says: "Limit desires"; Hinduism says, "Give up desire for separate existence"; Buddhism says: "Cut the root of desire even for life"; Jesus says,

"Blessed are the renounced in spirit." Lippmann would limit desires, so that in a world that is sure to disappoint, you will not be disappointed, for you have not asked too much; Hinduism would get rid of desire for separate personality by passing into the desireless Brahman; Buddhism would rid men of sorrow by cutting the root of suffering, namely, desire for life itself, thereby attaining Nirvana, which is the state of "the snuffed-out candle." Jesus would get rid of desire at the level of the self by replacing it with a higher desire of love to himself, thus bringing in a kingdom of higher values.

Lippmann ends in a disillusionment toward the world; Hinduism ends in a losing of the world and of personality in the impersonal Brahman; Buddhism ends in the extinction of the world and of personality; Jesus ends in a kingdom of positive values—the finding of one's life and the finding of a new world, the kingdom of God on earth. With the exception of Jesus, who ends in a final fullness, each ends in a final emptiness.

Jesus asks for the only possession we have —ourselves. Self-renunciation is far deeper than world-renunciation, for one may give up the world and not give up himself. I have seen many a sadhu who was poor in material things, but not poor in spirit, for if you crossed him, he would flash back in anger. No man is free until he is free at the center. When he lets go there, he is free indeed. When the self is renounced, then one stands utterly disillusioned, apart, asking for nothing. He anticipates the sorrows, the buffetings, the slights, the separations, the disappointments of life by their acceptance in one great renunciation. It is life's supreme strategic retreat. You can then say to life: "What can you do to me? I want nothing!" You can say to death: "What can you do to me? I have already died!" Then is a man truly free. In the bath of renunciation he has washed his soul clean from a thousand clamoring, conflicting desires. Asking for nothing, if anything comes to him, it is all sheer gain. Then life becomes one constant surprise.

The Greek philosophy tried to make a man invulnerable, but there was always an Achilles heel exposed where life would wound. The gospel begins at the cross, so that a man chooses to be utterly vulnerable—he wounds himself to death. Then he is impervious to wounds. You cannot defeat a man who has already accepted defeat; you cannot break Brokenness; you cannot kill a man who has chosen to die—he is now deathless. Buddha saw that the end of life was death and that it stopped there; Jesus saw that the beginning of life was death, and that it did not stop there but went on to an Easter morning.

I saw a very unhappy and angry bird beating

himself for hours against a glass, fighting with the reflection of himself. Then he suddenly stopped, listened, seemed to catch the call of the great out-of-doors, left off fighting with himself and flew away. After awhile I heard him singing out in the garden. Jesus comes to men who are fighting with themselves and with one another, full of clash and confusion, and in the words, "Deathless and happy is the man who is renounced in spirit," gives to them the call to the complete life. They listen, let go of themselves, enter into larger life and then in the garden of a restored paradise I hear them singing.

Deissmann tells of the custom in vogue at the time of Saint Paul, the manumission of a slave through the solemn rite of his purchase by a deity. The owner came with the slave to the temple, sold him there to the god, and received from the temple the purchase money which the slave had previously deposited there out of his savings. The slave then became the property of the god, but as against all the world he was a free man (*Saint Paul,* p. 141). This is something of what Jesus meant when he asked men, enslaved to themselves, to sell themselves to God, and then against all the world to step out free men.

The endeavor of modern men is to find "adjustment." But they usually adjust themselves so thoroughly to the material universe that they become all of a piece with it, and end in being a bit of mere mechanism. Jesus' first word is, Get out of adjustment on one level, to find a higher adjustment on a higher level. There you find real life. For the end of renunciation in spirit is not renunciation—it is receptivity: "Theirs is the kingdom of heaven," or "theirs is life." The self-renunciation ends in self-realization.

Everything belongs to the man who wants nothing. Having nothing, he possesses all things in life, including life itself. Nothing will be denied the man who denies *himself*. Having chosen to be utterly solitary, he now comes into possession of the most utterly social fact in the universe, the kingdom of God. "Religion is what a man does with his solitariness," says Whitehead. I would say, rather, that real religion begins when a man decides to be more solitary— he decides to withdraw utterly, he wants nothing of the world of man or of matter. He has God. That is enough. Now he is ready to come back into the world. He is washed clean of desires, now he can form new ones, from a new center and with a new motive. This detachment is necessary to a new attachment. Asceticism here is in order to an asepticism, and both in order to a new acceptance of the world. The fullest and most complete life comes out of the most completely empty life—an Easter morning comes out of a Calvary.

"Out of the deep a shadow,
  Then a spark;
 Out of the cloud a silence,
  Then a lark;
 Out of the heart a rapture,
  Then a pain;
 Out of the dead cold ashes
  Life again!"

But this attitude of renunciation needs correction. The fact is that every virtue needs correction by its opposite virtue. In the tropical forests of the East Indies is a flower which if taken by itself smells putrid, but mingled with the other scents of the forest smells pleasant. Many a virtue taken by itself smells bad! We have seen good people who were anything but attractive, for their virtues were uncorrected by opposite virtues. Renunciation in spirit ends in barren asceticism unless it is corrected and supplemented by world-participation. Jesus, in his amazing balance, provided that each of the virtues laid down in the Beatitudes was to be corrected by its opposite virtue. But he went further than that, for virtues may thus cancel each other instead of combining in a higher third. He saw that they combined into a higher virtue which summed up the best in each. Hence the Beatitudes go together, not in pairs, but in groups of three. This reminds us of Hegel's dictum that thought moves through three stages: thesis, antithesis, and synthesis. We find these

three stages in the first group: thesis—the renounced in spirit, the separated; antithesis—
those who mourn for the sake of others, who
feel the world's sorrow and pain and take it upon
themselves; synthesis—the meek who inherit the
earth. The renounced and the serving are combined and become the meek, who shall finally inherit and rule the earth.

"Blessed are those that mourn" is usually
taken to refer to those who, as in the Old Testament, mourned for the restoration of Israel, or,
in the more personal sense, those who mourn for
their sins and shortcomings—in either case an
anti-climax. But if it means an active sharing
and bearing of the world's hurt and sin in order
to cure it; if it means the kind of mourning that
Jesus manifested when he wept over the city of
Jerusalem, if there is the passion of the sorrow
of the cross in it, then it is not an anti-climax,
but a necessary counterpart and correction. The
first beatitude without the second ends in barren
aloofness, but with it, it ends in fruitful attachment. This verse cuts across those who would
say that religion is "an escape-mentality," a
means of escaping from pain and sorrow. Here
is religion deliberately choosing sorrow for itself
in order to cure it in others.

Blessed are those who feel for the world's sin
and sorrow—this is the very opposite of the
Hindu and Buddhist ideal of being unaffected
and aloof in spirit. Neither heat nor cold,

neither joy nor sorrow, neither the world nor
death affect them, they have gained the state
of the unaffected. Not so in the teaching of
Jesus. The renounced in spirit are affected and
affected deeply. Having been cleansed by renunciation they are now more sensitive than ever to
the world's pain. Glover tells us that in the
early days of Christianity the attempt was made
to Christianize the term and the attitude of
"apathy" undisturbedness, nonsuffering; but it
could not be done—not with a cross at the center
of the gospel.

These two beatitudes are the two directions of
a rhythmic heartbeat. If a heart beats in one
direction alone, it will beat itself to death; if it
beats in both, it will pour lifeblood into the
whole body. If there is renunciation alone, there
is spiritual suicide. On the other hand, if there
is participation in the world, a mourning for
others and that alone, without the withdrawal
from the world in spirit, then there is shallowness, or worse still, spiritual death. India suffers from the first; the West suffers from the
second.

I saw a High Court judge who had renounced
his office, his home, companionship—everything,
and who sat naked on the banks of the sacred
Ganges near his little hut in perpetual meditation. He would not speak to me lest it disturb
his quest for God-realization. He was the heart
of India beating only in the direction of aloof-

ness, and though he represented a heart, and must be respected as such, he poured no warm healing life into India's soul; and as for himself, one could see from the gathering blankness of his face that he was slowly committing spiritual suicide. He was nearing the life of the vegetable. He felt that this renunciation was the release of life, but one could see that it was only the reduction of life. On the other hand there are many Christians who are extraverts, who think only in terms of serving the world, and in the process their souls become shallow and empty. The world is too much with them for them to overcome it—they are overcome by it.

Luther, feeling a world-disgust, cried, "The world's an evil fellow; let us hope that God will soon end him," but Luther, usually right, missed it here, for the Christian cries, "The world's an evil fellow; I will renounce him in spirit," but then hastens to add, "The world is worth saving, and I will go any length of pain and mourning to redeem him." In the first beatitude there is the withdrawal with Jesus into the mount alone, in the second there is the joining of Jesus on the road to Calvary. The two Mounts are in these two verses: Mount of Olives—the mount of withdrawal from men, and Mount Calvary—the mount of drawing every man to your heart until it breaks. In the first you refuse to give yourself to any man, in the second you turn round and give yourself to every man.

Strange to say, in the gospel the first prepares for and brings on the second—the surrendered heart is the sensitive heart. When one is renounced in spirit, then he has "a heart at rest from itself to soothe and sympathize." Most people are so taken up with themselves and their own problems that the world's pain and sorrow cannot get to them. But when a man grows great by inward renunciation, then this expansion of soul brings its cross—he is hurt more widely and more deeply. Jesus dying on the cross of a broken heart is the direct result of Jesus withdrawing into the mountains and refusing to be made a king. Refuse a crown, and you will be crowned with thorns.

These two verses explain a seemingly hard saying of Jesus, a saying that has offended many: "If any man cometh unto me and hateth not his own father, and mother, and wife, and children, and brethren, and sisters, yea, and his own life also, he cannot be my disciple. Whosoever doth not bear his own cross, and come after me, cannot be my disciple" (Luke 14. 26, 27). The demand seems to be to hate or renounce every relationship or we cannot be his disciples. This taken alone would seem to mean a hard, unfeeling, unsocial asceticism of the Hindu type. But the second part of that statement saves it: "Whosoever doth not bear his own cross, and come after me, cannot be my disciple." Cross-bearing in the gospel was for others—the most completely social act that can be imagined, for at the cross Jesus took on himself everything that was not his. In these two verses he puts together the utterly unsocial act of hating father and mother and the utterly social act of bearing one's cross for them. He puts them together, for they belong together. We renounce in spirit our tenderest relationships, and then turn straight around and take on ourselves the deepest of bondage for their sakes, namely a cross. Without this second injunction the first would be hard, unfeeling, unsocial, but with it the whole becomes the most tender, the most feelingful, the most social act of which a human being is capable—he is willing to be crucified that others may live and live fully. He renounces the family in spirit, then returns to them with a cross on his shoulders to redeem them at any cost. Renunciation in spirit and return with a cross are Siamese twins: cut them apart and they will both bleed to death; keep them together and they live.

But the climax of the difficulty is not in the portion which demands that we hate father and mother. The climax is where Jesus put it, "yea, and his own life, or self, also." It is comparatively easy to give up father and mother and houses and lands; the rub comes at the place, "yea, and his own self also." The last thing we ever give up is ourselves. A present-day patriot cried out: "For the sake of my motherland I am willing to sacrifice my old mother; yea, and my children too; and, if necessary, I am willing to sacrifice myself also." He came last! Many a missionary has come to other lands and has given up everything—father and mother, houses and lands—everything except himself. Touch him and he is still touchy! The self is still there watchful of its own place and power and becomes the morbid center of spiritual problems. In the first beatitude Jesus strikes straight at this central problem, the self, and demands that we be renounced there before we can go on. The end of human life will be either the finished egotist or the perfect lover. The first beatitude is the end of the egotist, the second is the beginning of the lover. It is the nature of love to insinuate itself into the sorrows and sins of others. It is bound to mourn. It has the doom of bleeding on it. And rightly so, for "when we cease to bleed we cease to bless."

Now those that "mourn" are comforted. The strange thing happens that those who deliberately take on themselves trouble and pain in behalf of others find happiness—they are comforted. The most absolutely happy people of the world are those who choose to care till it hurts. The most miserable people of the world are those who center upon themselves and deliberately shun the cares of others in the interest of their own happiness. It eludes them. They save their lives and they lose them.

Comfort is made up of two words, *con,* "with," and *fortis,* "strength"—literally, "strengthened by being with." In choosing the way of the cross we find ourselves in an intimacy of companionship with Christ, who toils up that same road, and there in that way we hear words that make the heart sing amid its sacrifice. Then can the soul say, "Might one little drop of what I feel fall into hell, hell would be transformed into paradise." The comfort is not a sickly sentimental thing—it is not the wiping of tearful eyes, but the re-enforcing of the heart. The Beatitudes put no premium on mere mourning. Senseless suffering is not comforting—it is dulling, disintegrating. This, then, must be a suffering of a particular quality—a gladly chosen pain. This brings comfort. There is nothing so absolutely blessed as to be able to suffer well. The sorrow of the world brings death, but this sorrow brings life.

The first two beatitudes, corrected and supplemented by each other, result in a synthesis of the two and become a third, namely, the meek who inherit the earth. Meekness is usually considered weakness. Not here. It is a combination of two elements: the power and decisiveness that dare to be renounced in spirit, and the passion that so deeply feels the pain and sorrows of men that it gives itself in service. Those who want nothing from the world of men and things and yet are willing to share everything, because they feel so deeply, are the meek. As hydrogen and oxygen, two diverse elements, coming together produce an entirely new product, water, so the spirit of renunciation and the spirit of service coming together in a man make a new being, the most formidable being on earth—the terrible meek. They are terrible in that they want nothing, and hence cannot be tempted or bought, and in that they are willing to go any lengths for others because they feel so deeply. Christ standing before Pilate is a picture of the Terrible Meek. He could not be bought or bullied, for he wanted nothing—nothing except to give his life for the very men who were crucifying him. Here is the supreme strength—it possesses itself, hence possesses the earth. It is so strong, so patient, so fit to survive that it inherits the earth. No one gives the earth to those who have this terrible meekness; they come into it as their natural right, they inherit it because they have the blood of God in their veins. The type of character that will survive and rule the earth is the renounced and serving meek. All others are usurpers. The future of the world will be in the hands of those who serve and save the world. There will be a survival of the spiritually fit, and Jesus says that this type is spiritually fit to survive and to govern the earth. In the clash of the ideals of character this type comes out as the finally fit. "He that is greatest among you shall be your servant." And, vice versa, the servant of all shall become the greatest of all. He is not greatest who has the greatest number of servants, but he is greatest who serves the greatest number.

On a monument in Lahore is a statue of one of the British rulers of India, holding in one hand a pen and in the other a sword, with this inscription below it: "Will you be ruled by the pen or by the sword?" India, awakened to a national consciousness, was furious with this statue and the police had to guard it night and day lest it be torn down. The statue now stands unguarded because the inscription has been changed to, "By pen and by sword we have served you." India and the world will allow only those who serve to rule.

Nietzsche raved against this as slave morality, but Nietzsche with his so-called "master-morality" broke himself and his world to pieces, while Jesus, practicing this so-called slave-morality, goes straight to the throne of our moral universe. They tell me that all dogs were once wolves. One day a wolf came around behind man and said that he would give up his wild selfishness and would be meek and serve. He became a dog. The wild wolves are being slowly but surely exterminated, while the meek dogs are more and more inheriting the earth. Among mankind the same thing is happening—the militarists, the exploiters and the selfish are slowly but surely being exterminated as unfit to survive and the serving meek are inheriting the earth.

Jesus said a very puzzling thing when he declared that except we become as little children we cannot enter the kingdom of heaven—puzzling until science came along and showed us how wide was the application of the principle. Huxley once wrote to Kingsley and said: "It seems to me that science teaches in most unmistakable terms the Christian conception of entire surrender to the will of God. Science says, 'Sit down before the facts as a little child, be prepared to give up every preconceived notion, be willing to be led to whatever end Nature will lead you, or you will know nothing.'" If you are to reign as king in the kingdom of fact, you must be prepared to be a child and be led wherever the facts will lead you. Here science and religion come together in demanding the same spirit. In both science and religion the meek alone inherit the earth.

The earth is maya, illusion, says Hinduism. It is yours, says Jesus. When I walked out into the world the morning after I made my self-surrender I thought I had never before seen the world; the trees clapped their hands and all nature was atingle with joy and beauty. For the first time I knew that the earth was mine. I had inherited it. The gospel begins with a demand for self-renunciation and ends in a self-affirmation and in a world-affirmation.

The first three beatitudes strike at the aggressive attitudes of life. They show God's invasion of us, taking away our self-sufficiency, our very self-life, getting us ready for the most amazing offensive of love the world has ever seen. He disarms us in order to put entirely new weapons into our hands. Unless these first three verses become actual the rest of the Sermon on the Mount becomes impossible. The rub is not at the place of turning the other cheek; the rub is at the place of letting go the essential self. Do that, and turning the other cheek is a necessary and natural outcome.

To sum up: The renounced in spirit gain the kingdom of heaven, the mourners gain the kingdom of inner comfort, the meek gain the earth. So the world above, the world within, and the world around belong to this man. Wanting nothing he inherits all worlds.

CHAPTER IV

WHAT THEY ARE IN THEMSELVES—
CONTINUED

WE come now to the next trinity of beatitudes beginning with, "Blessed are they that hunger and thirst after righteousness; for they shall be filled." Jesus uses the strongest cravings—hunger and thirst—to characterize the passion for goodness which is found in the man who is bent upon perfection. This desire for righteousness becomes a hunger that eats up the lesser hungers of one's life, until the man himself is eaten up with this all-inclusive hunger. While the first three beatitudes strike at the aggressive attitudes toward life, they do not end there. They end, not in a quietism, but in a quest. And the quest for righteousness can now safely take place, after renunciation in spirit; the righteousness produced will not now be a self-righteousness, for the self has been laid down. Nothing is more beautiful than righteousness; nothing is more hideous than self-righteousness.

But even this righteousness, although purified by self-elimination, needs correction by the next beatitude, "Blessed are the merciful." Most righteous people are not merciful toward the failings and shortcomings of others. Their very passion for righteousness makes them hard. They are usually the Sinais where the law thunders forth, and if you touch that mount, you are thrust through with a dart of righteous precept. Righteousness unmodified by mercy is a hard, unlovely, Pharisaical, sour-visaged thing. A committee went to the station to meet the new minister whom they did not know by sight. They walked up to a man who alighted and asked him if he was the new incumbent. "No," he replied, "I am not. It is dyspepsia that makes me look this way." Righteousness without mercy produces an indigestion countenance. But nothing is more beautiful than the countenance of righteousness when there glistens upon it the tear of mercy. The voice of Sinai saying, "Thou shalt not" must be tempered by the voice of Calvary saying, "Father, forgive them." The students of a certain college were in suspense, for students at other colleges had been dismissed for doing the same thing that they had done. No word from the Scotch principal for two weeks. Then he arose in the chapel and said: "I wanted to dismiss you, but the voice of my Lord told me I must forgive you. I did not want to do it, but since he bids me I will." Every student was in tears. Sinai and Calvary spoke in the voice of the principal—and won! Righteousness that stood straight and towered, learned to stoop in mercy and conquered in the stooping.

But if the thirst for righteousness needs the

correction of mercy, then, vice versa, mercy needs the correction of righteousness. Mercy without righteousness is mushy. To be merciful toward the failings and sins of others without a moral protest at the heart of the mercy ends in looseness and libertinism. Either righteousness or mercy taken alone smells bad, but put together there is the breath of a heavenly scent upon them.

The two put together become the third: the pure in heart. Hunger for righteousness is the thesis, merciful toward others and their failings is the antithesis, the pure in heart is the synthesis. The best definition I know of purity of heart is just here: a passion for righteousness and a compassion for men—this is purity of heart. To be pure in heart is literally "undivided in heart"—undivided not only between good and evil, but between virtue and virtue. That heart is pure which does not divide any portion with any evil; but, more, it does not divide the virtues righteousness and mercy, giving itself alternately to one or to the other, but blends them into the blend of purity. It is controlled by both of them at once, so that the pure heart is righteously merciful and mercifully righteous. This kind of man sees God. The man who seeks law, and shows love, sees God.

It is well that the seeing of God is placed at this stage. Hinduism says, "Blessed are the renounced in spirit; they shall see God." The gospel says, "Blessed are those who are the renounced in spirit and suffer for others and thus become the meek who inherit the earth; who hunger and thirst after righteousness and are merciful to others, and thus become the pure in heart—these see God." The seeing of God is not through self-emptying alone, but the self-emptying is in order to a filling with the positive qualities of vicarious suffering, of meekness, of hunger and thirst after righteousness, of a tender mercy and a purity in heart. All these qualities fit one for finer relationships with man, so that God is seen, not apart from life, but in the midst of human relationships. Seeing God thus means fullness, not emptiness.

To see God in the midst of the ordinary! Then the sordid becomes the sacred, then penury need not snuff out poetry, then every bush is aflame with God and all life has meaning.

But the vision of God and his glory is not the last beatitude—the last set of beatitudes gives us a vision of man and his need: "Blessed are the peacemakers; for they shall be called sons of God." The Beatitudes do not leave us gazing at heaven; they end leaving us gazing at a scarred and warring earth. The purity becomes peacemaking. This purity, then, is not a purity that builds walls of separation about itself by taboos and exclusions—it is not a protected purity; it is a purifying force. It is not like the water that would throw round itself banks of exclusion and end in being a stagnant and festering pool; rather it is like the running brook that keeps pure by its very purifying. No purity is pure that is not purifying, and no virtue is virtuous that does not have the victorious in it. The renounced in spirit and the pure in heart are not called the sons of God until they become lovingly aggressive and become peacemakers.

This type of character, depicted in the first beatitudes, is now loosed upon the world in reconciliation. Having renounced themselves they are in a position to speak the authoritative word and breathe the authoritative spirit in self-asserting, and hence clashing, human situations. No one can be a peacemaker unless he has the spirit of disinterestedness.

And they are not merely peacemakers between man and man but peacemakers between man and God. Man is at enmity with God and is afraid of him. These peacemakers breathe such a winsomeness that men fall in love with God through them. This purified, loving aggression is often looked on by non-Christians as religious imperialism, a zeal for proselytism and a desire to manage other people's souls in their supposed interests. Hence, they say, there should be no conversions in religion. Let us admit that this beautiful spirit of reconciliation and peacemaking has often been corrupted into religious imperialism, into fussy intrusions, into proselytism that would compass land and sea to make one more proselyte. But while we repudiate these we must not let go this passion for sharing that lies at the heart of the gospel. It is not written merely in the commands of Jesus to go and share, it is written in the very constitution and make-up of the Christian soul. He cannot help it if he is to be Christian, for no life is Christian that is not Christianizing.

But this loving aggression pays the penalties of love and finds itself "persecuted" for this loving righteousness' sake. In a world where men love their chains and their clashes and think them a part of themselves, since they have been with them so long, anyone who disturbs them by loving aggression will find the world kicking back in persecution. Men hate to be disturbed— even for the better. The peacemakers must get used to the sight of their own blood. Woe unto you when all men speak well of you, said Jesus, for if they do then it proves that you have not disturbed men in the slightest. The peacemakers become the persecuted—the Quakers, probably the most Christian of any group of Christians, are hounded by a society that hates to be disturbed from war to peace; Gandhi goes to jail and Christ goes to his cross.

But the beatitude, "Blessed are those who are persecuted" adds something to "Blessed are the peacemakers" that was really necessary to complete the character. It is one thing to be a peacemaker, it is another thing to continue to be a peacemaker amid persecution. It is well that the peacemaker should know something of un-peace for himself. For, if he can have peace within amid the persecutions, he is then indeed a peacemaker. His peacemaking needs persecu-tion to make his continued peacemaking authori-tative and effective, for no man can speak on peace with moral authority unless he speaks out of the experience of peace amid disturbedness. Jesus is the Prince of Peace, for one thing be-cause he was a Prince when in the midst of persecutions. As Jesus speaks peace through the blood of his cross, so we cannot speak peace save through the blood of our own cross. Jud-son, after undergoing unspeakable sufferings while lying in stocks in prisons for months, gained his freedom and then asked the king of Burma for permission to go to a certain city to preach his gospel. "I am willing for a dozen preachers to go to that city," replied the king, "but not you. Not with those hands. My people are not fools enough to listen to and follow your words, but they will not be able to resist those scarred hands." Those scarred hands were authoritative.

Jesus said that the renounced in spirit have the kingdom of heaven and the persecuted peace-makers have the kingdom of heaven—why did he repeat this? Well, the kingdom of heaven only really belongs to the renounced in spirit as they become the persecuted peacemakers. That is, it is possessed not by negation—the renounced in spirit, but by affirmation—the loving aggression of the persecuted peace-sharers. The kingdom of heaven is not renunciation, but renunciation in order to reconcile.

The last beatitude, "Blessed are ye when men shall reproach you, and persecute you, and say all manner of evil against you falsely, for my sake. Rejoice and be exceeding glad: . . . for so persecuted they the prophets which were before you," adds something to the other two of the last trinity of beatitudes and completes them. It is not enough for one to be a peacemaker and be persecuted for his pains. He must know something of the meaning of the third, namely to "rejoice and be exceeding glad" amid the persecuted peacemaking. The thesis is the peacemaker, the antithesis is the persecution of the peacemaker, the synthesis is the joyous, persecuted peacemaker—the Happy Warrior.

In the Beatitudes we are told that we are to possess the kingdom of heaven, the kingdom within, the kingdoms of the earth. This life seems to conquer *all* kingdoms, but there is one left—the kingdom of pain. In this last beatitude Jesus says that the kingdom of pain also belongs to you. For those who follow this way do not merely bear pain, or escape it, or submit to it—they *use* it! They rejoice and are exceeding glad—*in spite of*. "Life is suffering—

escape it," says Buddhism. "Life brings suffering—use it," says Jesus. The minstrel of Ascalon went into battle with his harp aloft. So we!

I saw an eagle in the Himalayas when a storm struck it. I expected it to be dashed to the earth by the fury of the storm. Instead the eagle set its wings in such a way that, when the storm struck it, it arose above the storm. It did not bear the storm, or try to escape it. It used it to go higher. The set of the wings did it. Here in these Beatitudes Jesus is telling us how to give a set to the soul so that when trouble and pain strike one, he simply rises on the fury of it. Pain can dull one, it can also drive one—into higher altitudes. I knew of an aged saint who was so filled with a living joy that when he was coming out of a railway train and the jolting threw him against the sides, it jolted "hallelujahs" out of him! He had them within him so that the jolting simply brought them out!

There was the ancient custom of stretching wires between the towers of a castle to make an Æolian harp. When there was calm there was no music, but when the storm raged, then from the harp came exquisite melody. The harp used the storm—it turned its fury into melody. Jesus opens this possibility to man. He who has learned the secret of using pain is now safe, for he can stand anything that can happen to him. He snatches the club from the hand of circumstances which would smash his head and turns it into a baton with which to lead the music that breaks forth from within. Like the lily that transforms into beauty the muck and slime in which it grows, so he transforms hate into hallelujahs and misery into melody. This possibility throws open to man an utterly victorious way of life. "The Stoic bears, the Epicurean submits, the Christian alone exults." That pain can be creative, contributive, is the teaching of Jesus. Said a wise Christian to another, "My son, it does not matter what you lose provided you offer it up alongside of the sacrifice of Christ." Another puts it this way: "The primrose path of life is quickly overrun with briars, and if we must be pierced with thorns, it is more kingly to wear them as a crown."

The secret of this last beatitude is in the first beatitude. You overcome the pains of life by anticipating them beforehand. You inflict upon yourself the supreme pain of a self-renunciation—what can lesser pain do after that? Luke adds to this beatitude the words: "Blessed are ye . . . when men shall separate you"—you can meet that, for you have separated yourself beforehand by a self-surrender. This lesser separation is nothing—you have made the supreme one. You have pulled the sting out of the lesser deaths by inwardly consenting to die.

"You are always talking about life; don't you ever think about dying? Don't you know that you will have to die?" said a very able Buddhist in a somewhat peeved tone.

"No," I replied, "I do not think about dying. Why should I? When one has long ago inwardly consented to die, he can forget all about dying and can think about living. But even if death should come, I am like the bird on the twig of the tree when the storm tries to shake it off. 'All right,' the bird says to itself, 'shake me off. I've still got wings.'"

Let death shake me from my earthly twig, I still have another alternative—I still have wings, so that whether in life or death one can still rise above his circumstances.

Jesus' way of life is a way of death—the cross. The Swiss have a story of the man in ancient days who, when there was no way through the enemy line, gathered all the hostile spears he could reach, let them pierce his own breast, and falling down held them there to allow his comrades to walk over his prostrate body to victory through the way thus opened. When one consents to the way of the cross, he gathers up into his heart all the spear-points of trouble and sorrow that life can point at him and holding them there, everything within him can now march on to victory over the prostrate form of his consented death.

"We do not want a cross, we want joy. Krishna with the lute is a better symbol of religion than Christ with a cross," said a European theosophist to me one day. Yes, we do want joy, but not a cheap joy—we want joy through a cross.

The Beatitudes, which begin with a demand for a renunciation of spirit, end in a leaping "for joy" (Luke 6. 23). The beatitude of the modern man begins with a self-sufficiency of spirit and ends in a dull disillusionment and cynicism. One ends in an exhaustion of spirit, the other ends in an exhilaration of spirit.

The secret of all this is a phrase in the last beatitude—"for my sake." All of this is to be worked out in living fellowship with this Person. These, then, are not dead precepts to be worked out for duty's sake, but a living fellowship which is to be worked out for love's sake. Love for a Person is the life of these precepts—it infuses new life into the dead body of doctrine. Everything in the Sermon on the Mount is worked out from this place—love for a holy Person. Without this the Sermon on the Mount is impossible. The weary feet of duty cannot climb such heights but the winged feet of love can tread these heights—and higher!

The first beatitude begins with a supreme losing—oneself; the last beatitude ends with a supreme finding—Himself. Nothing now can be loss with this gain. A man worked hard for years to get money to build a house and furnish it so that he could marry the woman of his choice. The great day had come and he started on his honeymoon feeling that the sun of his happiness had

arisen in the heavens to stay there forever. But
at a certain station a telegram was handed him
which read: "Your home burned—a total loss."
He turned pale and his lips trembled. All the
labor of those years gone in a moment! His
wife looked over his shoulder, read the telegram,
thought a moment, then looked into his face and
smiled and said, "Well, never mind, dear; we
still have one another." When persecution sets
in, when we are separated from the company of
men, when death robs us of a dear face, when
life crashes around us, then, in spite of all, we
can say, "Well, Jesus, we still have one another."
"For my sake" transforms everything.

But it not only transforms loss into gain, it
transforms problems into possibilities. We can
do anything through this inner fellowship with
Christ. The Sermon on the Mount is possible
because the Companion of the Valley is with
you and in you. That Companionship, however,
is not merely a comfort, it is a challenge. "You
are so free," said a Moslem barrister to me one
day. "Now I have my regular religious rules to
go through with every day, but you do not have
any such rules. You are free—too free." I
acknowledged that, as a Christian, I was not
under a set of rules, but that, on the other hand,
I was under a far deeper bondage than he ever
dreamed of. I was never free from this inward
impulsion, duty was never done, for love has no
limits, and attainment was never accomplished,

for love was always opening new doors. In a legal code you do the deed and it is sufficient. In this the deed is not sufficient—every thought, every impulse is held by this inner grip of love.

But this love is liberty. "The water that I shall give him shall become in him a well of water springing up," said Jesus. It is difficult to give without weakening others, without taking away their spontaneity, their self-reliance, their very souls. Hence many think that a religion of grace is weakening. But not so in Jesus. He accomplishes the almost impossible. "The water that I shall give"—the thing that I impose on him, shall become in him a well, something that springs up from within him. The imposition from without becomes an impulse from within. His giving us water from without seems artificial—it is really artesian. Only the Divine could think of a way in which I can by one stroke find self-submission and self-expression. But Jesus is that way. "For his sake," I find, in the end, to be for my sake. His injunctions and my interests are one.

It was said of Jesus: "He comported himself in duty as on a holiday." So we!

CHAPTER V

WHAT THEY ARE TO THE WORLD

AFTER laying his first emphasis on what this new type is, Jesus proceeds to describe the effect of such living—they become "the salt of the earth" and "the light of the world" (see Matthew 5. 13-16).

In what world-encompassing terms he now speaks! It sounds like the stately march of cosmic music. If man is too small to catch its wonder and march to its rhythmic beats, he knows that man must live forever in his own discords and be doomed to littleness and to the tom-toming of his own desires. He has nothing smaller to offer. It is this or nothing. The sheer daring of telling a group of ex-fishermen on a hillside in a remote corner of the world that they were to become the one hope of the world! That they would save it from moral putrefaction and from moral darkness! It is breath-taking. These statements about being the salt of the earth and the light of the world are either cosmic or comic. Two thousand years of history demonstrates that real Christian character has been in very fact the salt of the earth and the light of the world.

The first beatitude insists on self-renunciation; now Jesus offers self-expression in worldcompassing terms. He can make that offer now, for the kind of self-expression that has a renunciation at its center is safe—for the man and for the world.

The action of salt is twofold: it saves from putrefaction and it saves from insipidity. It saves from putrefaction. One of the ancients said that "what the soul is to the body the Christian is to the world"—take away the soul and the body is a decaying carcass; keep it there and the body is a beautiful organism. "If God Almighty lets the British Empire live, it is because of men like Colonel W——," said a Hindu nationalist to me in reference to the Christian character of a British engineer. His character was salt. "If bribery and corruption have been abolished from the public life of this state, it is because of the character and example of two Indian Christians," said a Moslem Prime Minister of a leading Indian state, speaking of two Indian Christians in high office under him. When there were Hindu-Moslem riots in this state, the Hindu Maharaja sent for the Prime Minister and said to him: "In this crisis you listen to whatever M—— tells you to do. I have absolute confidence in his character and integrity." Here an Indian Christian by the sheer force of his character was the virtual ruler of the state in that crisis. "We have had to stop using bad language," said a landowner of high caste, "for if we don't, then none of these Chris-

tians from the outcastes will work for us." The
greatest asset for stability that Britain has had
in India during these last few turbulent years
has not been the standing army, but the Christian character of Lord Irwin, the late viceroy.
An ardent congressman who was fighting the
British government said to me of Lord Irwin,
"He is a Christian to his finger tips." It is confidence in a kind of Christianity that reaches
clear to the finger tips in Lord Irwin that has
held the situation steady. "Isn't Gandhi the perfect Christian?" I get again and again at the
question hour. Agree with the question or not,
nevertheless of one thing we are sure, that it is
the Christian elements in Mahatma Gandhi's
character that have held India to nonviolence.
On the side of the Indian Gandhi was the salt
of the situation that kept it from putrefying
into violence, as on the side of the British Lord
Irwin was the salt that kept the confidence of
the Indian alive in British character. "My
father, my father, the chariots of Israel and the
horsemen thereof," cried the disciple of Elijah
as his master was being taken away. He saw
that Elijah by his very character had been the
standing army of Israel—the chariots of Israel
and the horsemen thereof. He was the country's
safety.

The Christian is to be salt not merely to save
life from moral putrefaction. He is to save life
from losing its taste and becoming insipid. The

gospel is the greatest adventure in faith in life and its worth-whileness that the world has ever seen. "I am come that they might have life, and that they might have it more abundantly," is its central and nerve-giving note. It is this sense of victorious vitality that puts nerve and courage into life which otherwise grows gray on our hands. In East and West men are suffering from failure of nerve. On the whole, religion in the East is suffering from a vast failure of nerve, of world-weariness, of personality-weariness and of life-weariness. All is Maya, illusion. Life has become tasteless and insipid. Escape it. It is this that has been back of the lack of progress in the East. If the East is now alive and is yearning for fuller and freer life, it is because the salt of Christian ideas has touched the situation and has given hope and taste again to life. For at the heart of the gospel is an undiscouraged and an undiscourageable dynamic. It is irrepressibly hopeful and full of faith in God, in people, and in life itself.

But it is not in the East alone that futilitarianism has spread the shadow of its wings over the souls of men. In the West "some have fled to hell," where they were

> "Gratified to gain
> That positive eternity of pain,
> Instead of this insufferable inane."

Life runs through its resources and there is

nothing left except "this insufferable inane." They live in what has been called "a generally devaluated world," so there is nothing left to live for. Lippmann quotes Canby as saying that "modern youth at the age of 7 saw through their parents and characterized them in a phrase; at 14 they saw through education and dodged it; at 18 they saw through morality and stepped over it; at 20 they lost respect for their home towns, and at 21 they discovered that our social system is ridiculous. At 23 the autobiography ends because the author had run through society to date and does not know what to do next." Hegasias wrote after Hedonism, or the pursuit of the pleasurable, had had its vogue in Greece, and he was called significantly "the persuader to die." It was the only thing left, for life after pursuing the pleasurable had turned insipid.

Anatole France worshiped at the shrine of the cult of Beauty and said: "All I desire is that at the end a beautiful woman shall close my eyes in death." Has his worship of Beauty put taste into life? Listen to what he said: "I cannot remember that I have had a single happy day in my life, except perhaps when I was a little child." His beauty had turned to ashes. "Oh, hell!" cries many a modern youth—and he thinks he is swearing, when all that he is doing is unconsciously to reveal the fact that he has nothing but expended resources within, and that he is living in the hell of the insufferable inane. In giving rein to passion he grasps at the lurid sunset and finds that he has grasped the dark! He has gained the kingdom of rot. In the New Testament the man with the one talent went off and "dug a hole in the ground." The end of his life's work was an empty hole. Many are going off and doing nothing more than digging holes in the ground. The end is emptiness, insipidity, futility.

Jesus puts taste into life. "Let down the curtain, the farce is done," cried an actor as death approached. "Raise the curtain to fuller scenes, life has just begun," cries the Christian whether living or dying. In either case he lives —he lives! Jesus saves us from cynicism as well as from sin, from the losing of the nerve as well as the losing of the soul.

Jesus now changes the figure to describe the amazing influence of this kind of character: "Ye are the light of the world." He has to change the figure to describe the full impact of Christian character upon life. The action of salt is silent, pervasive, hidden, unseen; the action of light is open and manifest—the most openly expressed thing imaginable. The influence of Christian character is to be twofold, a silent, hidden and pervasive thing reaching into the very fiber of men's thought and outlook; and it is to be open, lighting the outer life of men and their affairs. But it is to be inward and per-

vasive before it is to be outward—we are to be
salt before we can be light. No man can shine
in obviousness unless he is willing to permeate in
obscurity. Many of us would like to be light, but
we are unwilling to work like salt, unseen, un-
noticed, unapplauded. We have, what Bishop
Quayle called in quaint but questionable Latin,
"Ichus publendi"—the itch for publicity. We
have no real passion to change things where
change really matters, namely, within. The
Christianity of the present day is hurt by a desire
to be light coupled with an unwillingness to be
salt. It is suffering from an outwardism that is
more interested in statistics than in states of
heart and mind. One of the greatest difficulties
I have in my work is the demand of the shallow
that my work among the educated classes of
India shall be light, shall be seen in statistics, reportable in church councils. They
are impatient at the idea of our gospel being
salt, silent and changing the inner spirit and
attitudes of a nation. Some day I hope that it
will be light; in the meantime I am content if
it be salt.

As Jesus talks to us in these breath-taking
terms about what we are to mean to the world
he couples with it a most pointed warning that
we may mean nothing, worse than nothing, for
the salt may lose its savor and the light may be
snuffed out under bushels. He says: "Ye are the
salt of the earth, but if the salt have lost its

savor, wherewith shall it [the world] be salted?"
He puts it more pointedly in Luke: "Salt therefore is good; but if even the salt have lost its
savor." This presupposes that the outside world
has lost its savor—that is a foregone conclusion;
but sometimes "even the salt" loses its savor.
Where, then, is there seasoning for tasteless life
in the world? The fact is that life in the world
has lost its savor. Men go from thing to thing
and from thrill to thrill to put seasoning back
into dull, tasteless life. Jesus challenges those
who are vainly endeavoring to find seasoning for
life to find it in some way other than his way—
wherewith shall it be seasoned?—and the ages
of fruitless endeavor answer, Yes, wherewith?
It is quite true, says Jesus, that the world does
not have it. But it may also be true of you—
then you are good for nothing. He knew that
religion which would save the world from futility might itself become the most absolutely futile thing in the world, as futile as tasteless
salt. In that case men cast it out and tread it
under their feet. Ofttimes the rejection of religion is not because of the wickedness of men,
but because of the worthlessness of religion. In
South India there is a "Self-Respect Movement"
among the lower castes. It is anti-caste, and in
a way anti-religious. They say that its adherents
run into the millions. It has an organ printed
in English and Tamil entitled *Revolt*. This title
is printed in red letters beginning with a small

"r," each letter getting larger until the huge, final "t."

"That looks like a conflagration," I remarked to one of them, "you begin with a small spark and at the end you are a huge flame."

He replied that that was the meaning. Men had lost respect for religion that gave them no self-respect. The desertion of churches is often not so much because men are irreligious, as because the churches themselves are insipid and futile. An English public man of letters remarked concerning a certain church in Assam, "This church was dedicated to official Christianity—and emptiness." The one followed the other.

When religion stands for things as they are, then men will let them stand as they are—empty. If there is not the sense of dealing with real issues in them, then men will let them alone as constituting no real issue to them. Cattle and buffaloes will travel long distances to lick the lumps of crystal salt, but they will not go two steps to a saltless crystal. The problem is not to get people into the church, but to get salt into the churches. Get it there and the people will come.

The Jerusalem Conference made many great advances, but I believe it made one false step when it urged Christians to join with other religions against the growth of skepticism and secularism. Certainly, we Christians cannot go back to the old attitudes of aloofness from other religions. We must co-operate with them in every possible way to maintain a spiritual interpretation of life against a secularistic. But if this exhortation that we co-operate with other religions against the growth of skepticism goes on the assumption that any religion is better than no religion, then I demur. Religion of itself is not necessarily a good thing—it may be a bane or a blessing to men. In the sacred name of religion men have fought and hated and lusted and exploited. Some of the worst pages of human history have been written by religion in East and West. I refuse to protect religion that will not protect man. Religion may be and often has been a bar to human progress. Voltaire pouring out his invectives upon superstitions really did a service to religion in the West by helping to purge it. India needs an Indian Voltaire. Shall we protect religious systems against skepticism when those systems lie as an incubus on the souls and bodies of men? Especially when that skepticism is a protest in behalf of men against a system? Trace back the economic and social evils in the East and you will find almost everyone of them rooted in religious custom.

"We will never make any progress until we drop all the pundits into the Ganges," said a Hindu student to me one day.

"If the pundits and the priests block reform,

we will shut them up in a room and lock them there," said a leading Hindu nationalist.

The orthodox held a meeting of protest and the Congress people surrounded the meeting and yelled, "Inquilab Zindabad!"—Long live Revolution!—a cry that had hitherto been cried against the British government, but was now being cried against religion that backed social wrongs. There was more real religion in the cry of the nationalists who stood for the people against the system than in the protest of the orthodox who stood for a system against the people. If I must choose—thank God I need not—but if I must choose, I would rather choose irreligious humanism than inhuman religion. "Lilies that fester smell worse than weeds"—religion corrupted is most evil-smelling. Jesus announced with sorrow that the Temple, the ancient depository of religion, must be destroyed in order that real religion might live. No, the Jerusalem Conference was more sentimental than sensible if its request meant for us to stand with all religions against the skepticism that was searching these systems in behalf of human rights and human progress. It is often a sure instinct for men to cast out savorless salt and tread it under their feet. I have found more skepticism in India this last year than I have in the previous twenty-four years I have been here. And it is a healthy skepticism, purging the minds of men from superstitions. Nor do I ask for special treatment for the religion I hold. It too must be exposed to this demand for reality, and if men honestly find it tasteless, they will, and should, cast it out. I have no final fears, for though Christianity has often been the enemy of Christ, nevertheless I believe there is enough salt in Christ to resalt savorless Christianity. "I have had no encouragement in my efforts at reforms for the laboring man from any of the religions of India except Christianity. If I were religious at all, I could only be religious as a Christian," said the leading Hindu labor leader of India. Such a statement and many like it give me hope, but not a false hope, for the warning of the Master rings in our ears that tasteless religion, even if it is among his own followers, will be cast out and trodden under the feet of men.

There was the further warning against hiding the light under the bushel (Matthew 5. 15). The bushel is the symbol of trade, of business— the lighted life is put under the business with the consequence that business mentality and methods and preoccupations snuff out the lighted life. That which was to have been the light of the world is snuffed out by worldliness. The bushel is also the instrument of measurement, and Jesus gives us the semihumorous picture of the man trying to measure the light of the candle by a bushel and putting out the light in the process. Our desire for statistics, for tabulation of spiritual results, is like the man putting the bushel over the candle to measure its light. In the process many a spiritual movement is quenched. We are inundated with questionnaires that are really refined and well-graduated bushels to measure the light of the gospel as it shines from very human candlesticks. These candles often have to be relighted by prayer and rededication after the embarrassing and impossible process of having one's light reduced to tables and statistics. "The kingdom of God cometh not with observation . . . the kingdom of God is within you," said Jesus, but we, sensebound as we are, say that the kingdom of God does come by observations and inquiries, and that it is to be found within the statistical tables! And the light, so well-measured, goes out.

It is possible to put your light on the top of the bushel, not under it, to make of your business a candlestand, a means through which your Christian life shines. You may throw open the doors of your business in the morning as one who throws open the doors of opportunity for the service of God and man; and you may handle your ledgers with as much sense of sacred mission as the minister handles the Bible in the pulpit. When Lord Irwin, the great Christian viceroy, said at the close of an interview: "I may not see you out here again, but I would like you to know that you and I are working for the same purposes," he meant that he had the same sense of commission as I, a missionary had, and that he was using the office of viceroy, with all its perplexities and responsibilities, as a means of letting his Christian life shine. And it did.

"A city set on a hill"—a life elevated above its surroundings cannot help but be elevating. Some of us living in spiritual depression try to give forth spiritual expression. The result is unnatural and strained. Life raised, naturally raises its light. A life higher than its surroundings cannot be hid. The life is the light. It is the nature of light to shine, of salt to permeate, of the Christian to share. When the Christian does not share his spiritual life with others, he not only denies his Lord, he denies his own life.

"It shineth to all that are in the house." Religion is to be as free as light. When Mrs. Besant, the head of the Theosophists, tried learnedly to prove that there was an "esoteric Christianity," she quoted texts, but forgot the texture of the Christian soul. It is open, frank, and shines to all that are in the house. "The Gospels exclude none, except those who exclude themselves." There are no snobberies in the gospel, not even spiritual snobberies.

CHAPTER VI

WHAT THEY ARE TO THE PAST

WE come now to one of the most important statements that ever fell from the lips of Jesus: "Think not that I am come to destroy the law, or the prophets: I am not come to destroy, but to fulfill." Evidently, what he had been saying, the spirit and the directness of it, made his hearers feel their Jewish universe begin to shake and reel as by an earthquake. What relevance had elaborate and minute Temple rites and ceremonies after this? The center of religion was being shifted from the Temple to the heart and from the Jew as a Jew to man as man. As the shifting took place his hearers could feel their Jewish souls turn pale within them. So he assures them: "Think not that I am come to destroy: . . . I am come to fulfill." He would gather up and preserve any beauty, any truth, any goodness of the past and fulfill or complete it in himself.

This statement—"I came not to destroy, but to fulfill," is a generic statement. It is locally applied to the Law and the Prophets, but is capable of a wider application to truth found anywhere. Had this statement not been in the Gospels, our attitude toward other cultures and other religions must have been as iconoclastic as Islam. When, now, we go to another culture and to another religion, our whole mental attitude is changed—we can look for the good. We know that any truth, any goodness, or any beauty found in other cultures is a ray of "that . . . Light which lighteth every man that cometh into the world." Christ has been there before us, though unrecognized and unknown. In the words of Augustine, "That which is now called the Christian religion existed among the ancients and has never failed since the beginning of the human race until Christ came in the flesh, whence the true religion which was already in existence began to be called Christian" (Retract 1. 13). God intends to save a race. So before the final revelation in Christ we find ideas being implanted in the human mind wherever it would open in order that men could understand them when they came in their perfection and completion. It is a law of the mind that we cannot understand an absolutely new thing. It must be related to something that went on before. Without this period of preparation we could have understood the gospel no better than a rabbit could understand higher mathematics. "None can receive a revelation which is unrelated to his education, his habits of thought, and experience of life," says Dean Inge. He reminds us that the second-century apologists and the Christian Platonists not only acknowl-

edged their obligations to pagan philosophy, but
admitted divine inspiration in Heraclitus, Socrates, and Plato. As Clement of Alexandria
said, "The river of Christianity has received
many affluents."

Christ will gather up in himself all partial
truth and preserve it. When I come to another
civilization I know in my heart of hearts that
Christ is not the enemy but the preserver of any
fine trait or tendency or teaching in that civilization. In him the prayer-wheel of the Buddhist becomes the "pray without ceasing" of the
gospel. The idol of the old faiths becomes "the
express image of his Person." The individualistic karma of the old becomes the transferred
karma of the cross. The Sangha of the Buddhist and the caste brotherhood of the Hindu
become the brotherhood of man, the kingdom
of God in the Gospels. The sacrifice of the animal
to the Divine becomes the Divine self-sacrifice.
The preserved mummy of the old becomes the
resurrected Christ of the new. The happy hunt-
ing ground of the Red Indian becomes the land
of everlasting fellowship and service. The many-
handed gods of the old become the ever-helpful
Father of the new. The passivity of the Buddhist becomes the poised Passion of the Christ.
The world-renunciation of the Hindu and the
Buddhist becomes the self-renunciation of the
Gospels. The three gods of the Hindu pantheon
who are called one, become the one God who

is manifested as Trinity. The peace of indifference of the Hindu becomes the peace of the poised heart that has rest from itself to soothe and sympathize. The yearning for the incarnate of the Gita is fulfilled in the Incarnate of the gospel. The expectancy of the coming of "the spotless incarnation" of all Hinduism becomes the Crystal Christ as historic fact. The yellow robe of world-renunciation becomes the Seamless Robe of world-redemption.

He came to fulfill. He came to fulfill the desire of the Egyptians for immortality by himself rising from the dead and saying, "I am the resurrection and the life"; the naturalness of the Greeks, by making his way of life a well, springing up from within unto everlasting life; the love of the Romans for authority by assuming an authority over life that goes to the last thought and to the last motive; the craving among the Buddhists for the cessation of suffering by the turning of suffering into a song; the truth of submission in Islam by demanding that every thought be brought under captivity to the obedience of Christ; the reverence of the Chinese for ancestors and for elders by making the world a human family with God as our Father and all men as our brothers; the passion of the Japanese for loyalty by making loyalty to himself and to the Beloved Community the very center of his gospel; the desire of the Hindus for unity with the Divine by offering to men that unity with God expressed in the words, "I in them and thou in me, that they may be perfected into one"—Christ, God, man—perfected into one!

All great systems of thought and religion break up into one of three accordingly as they emphasize one of the three constituent parts of a man's personality: mind, emotion, and will. The three outstanding German thinkers illustrate this: Hegel—the way of the mind; Schleiermacher—the way of the emotion; Kant—the way of the will. The Hindus give the three ways of salvation as: The Gyana Marga—the way of knowledge, or mind; the Bhakti Marga—the way of devotion, or emotion; the Karma Marga—the way of works, or will. They give you the choice of any one of the three ways. Jesus is all three ways in one: "I am the Way"—a way of acting, of doing, of going—the Karma Marga; "I am the Truth"—the way of knowing—the Gyana Marga; "I am the Life"—the way of emotion— the Bhakti Marga. When we truly live in him, we are in all three ways at once. And we must have all three. No one of them can suffice. The Gita does give all three ways and seems to combine them, but not as in Christ where the Person becomes the incarnation and realization of the three ways. The Gita has the idea of the three ways, but not the realization in the one Person.

The Greeks emphasized three great things: Goodness, Truth and Beauty. Jesus fulfilled all three: "I am the Way"—Goodness; "I am the Truth"—Truth; "I am the Life"—Beauty.

Physically we live by three things: food, air, and exercise. Spiritually we live by three things: by spiritual food—the assimilation of the mind of Christ in the Word; by spiritual breathing—prayer is breathing, breathing out the bad air of our sins and troubles to God, and breathing in the good air of his grace and strength and inner healing; spiritual exercise—service to others. Jesus meets all three of these growth needs of man: "I am the Way"—exercise; "I am the Truth"—food; "I am the Life" —air. He also meets these growth needs by his own example. Three things he did by habit: "He stood up to read the Scriptures, as his custom was"—assimilation, food; "He went out into the mountain to pray, as his custom was"— prayer, breathing; "He taught them again, as he was wont"—exercise. He thus meets the growth needs of man in a twofold way: He *did* these three things himself, so he met them by way of example; he *was* these three things, so he met them by imparting himself.

The intellectually inclined demand that religion be Philosophy. A thoughtful Hindu sent up this question: "As Christianity has no system of philosophy behind it, but has only a God of ethical conduct, how is it suited to the philosophically-minded Hindu race?" On the other hand, those who are will-minded demand that religion be Ethics. Those who are feeling-minded demand that it be Realization. It is true that the gospel is not a philosophy. It is a fact. The order is: first, fact; then philosophy about that fact. Jesus presents the fact of himself as the gospel. About that Fact more philosophies have been written than about any other fact. They fill our libraries. But the gospel is not founded on the uncertain and often contradictory deductions of philosophy. Jesus is more than philosophy, he is more than ethics, he is more than emotional realization. He is all three: I am the Way—Ethics; I am the Truth—Philosophy; I am the Life—Realization. He meets the needs of the man of action, the man of thought, and the man of feeling. He meets the whole man.

They asked him what was the greatest commandment, and he said, "Thou shalt love the Lord thy God with all thy heart [the emotional nature], with all thy soul [the volitional nature], with all thy mind [the intellectual nature], . . . and with all thy strength [the physical nature]." The whole man was to love God. "Strength" may mean physical strength, but it may also mean the strength of the emotion, the strength of the mind, the strength of the will. Some love with the strength of the emotion and the weakness of the mind—the sentimentalist in religion; others love with the strength of the mind and the weakness of the emotion—the intellectualist in religion; others love with the strength of the will and the weakness of the emotion—the man of iron in religion, righteous but not winsome. Jesus said that we were to love with the strength of all three—that makes the Christian. Christ himself is all three: I am the Way—will; I am the Truth—mind; I am the Life—emotion. He thus came not to destroy, but to fulfill our real humanity. Salvation according to the New Testament is "health." To "be saved" is to "be whole." It is the affirmation, the completion, the fulfillment of man by being made in the image of the Man, Christ.

Paul says an interesting thing: "If any man is in Christ there is a new creation; the old things are passed away; behold, they [the old things] are become new." Old things are passed away —nothing, absolutely nothing except Christ, is necessary for salvation for the Christian— neither law, nor sacrifices, nor circumcision, nor any other thing. They have all passed away. But lo, they are become new! The law which has passed away has now become new as a law written, not on tables of stone, but on the heart by the constant and growing impact of the mind of Christ. Sacrifices have passed away, only to become new in that we must now offer the sacrifices of our own very selves. For the man who has come out of Hinduism into a following of Christ, everything of the old is gone—not one thing of the old is necessary for his salvation— he has all in Christ. And yet all things become

new. Rebirth which was posited as a necessity
in order to attain salvation is gone, but it has
become new in new-birth, for new-birth fulfills
the necessity underlying rebirth. Monism—the
absolute identification of the human and the divine has passed away, but it has become new in
a union with God so deep that life flows into
life, purpose into purpose, mind into mind, a
union of life and love. Meditation upon abstract
and passionless Being has passed away, but it
has returned as communion—constant communion in the heart with God. World-renunciation
has passed away, but it has come back new in
self-renunciation.

Christ is the end of all things—and the beginning of all things! They die with him at the
cross and live with him in the resurrection.
Christ saves not merely the individual soul, he
saves every fine trait in national character, every
truth embedded in dead forms, every partial con-
cept in thought systems. He saves the past, by
not stopping at the past. He carries it on to
completion.

But not only does Christ fulfill all that is in
the past, the Christian is to do the same. He is
to be the universal character. Jesus brings this
out when he says that they are to be the salt
of the earth and the light of the world. The
Hebrew word was Righteousness—salt; the
Greek word was Illumination—light. Jesus
said that his disciples were to be both Righteous-

ness and Illumination—they were to sum up the finest in each national quest and genius. If the Hebrew word was Righteousness and the Greek word was Illumination, the Buddhist word is Desirelessness, the Hindu word is Unity, the Confucianist word is Superior, the Japanese word is Loyalty, the Christian word is Life. Because the Christian's word is Life, he sums up all the lesser qualities of life found in each national bent and genius. "Of the twain—Jew and Gentile—they were to make one new man," said Paul. The Christian character is tied up to no special food, no special dress, no special temperament, no special nationality, no special culture, no special time-element in history. The real Christian inherits the earth. "Man survives by the catholicity of his appetite," the Christian survives by the catholicity of his culture and his absorbing power. Add up all the fine qualities that inhere in each nationality— the thoroughness of the Teuton, the sturdy independence of the Scandinavian, the truth-loving of the Anglo-Saxon, the graciousness of the Latin, the passion for sharing of the Slav, the music-loving gaiety of the Negro, the practical-mindedness of the Chinese, the loyalty of the Japanese, the deep mysticism of the Indian— when you add all these together in the sum total you have something akin to Christian character. But Christian character is all these—plus. It can assimilate all, for it is an affirmation, not a denial. And yet it is not a composite. The plant reaches down into the soil and takes out elements akin to its own nature. But the end is not a patchwork of heterogeneous elements. It is a new living thing, for the laws of the life of the plant determine the disposition of the elements taken from the soil. Thus the gospel reaches down into the soil of each nation and picks out elements akin to its own nature. But here again the end is not a syncretism, for the law of life in Jesus Christ is the determining factor in the disposition of these assimilated elements. "Syncretism combines, eclecticisms pick and choose, but only life assimilates." The gospel repudiates syncretism, it refuses an eclecticism, but it does assimilate, for it is life.

But in its assimilations it discriminates. It does not take everything and it puts the more valuable first. Jesus said that they were to be salt before they were light. They had to be righteousness before they could be illumination. Now evil has invaded the whole personality— intellectual evil is error, emotional evil is suffering, the evil of the will is sin, the evil of the being is depravity. The center of the battle against evil is at the place of the will—sin. The battle of the mind is great, the battle of the emotion is greater, but the battle of the will is decisive. The worth of a man's personality is the worth of his will. The worth of a man's religion is determined by how much it controls his will. Righteousness is first and central in religion.

The Hebrew, then, is the foundation, not the Greek or the Hindu, for both of these claim that illumination, not righteousness, is first. A prominent Hindu editor puts it this way: "To the Hindu salvation is by knowledge. To one who knows, the question of sin does not arise. If this is too abstruse for the missionaries, Jesus would understand it when he said, 'Ye shall know the truth, and the truth shall make you free.'" But both the Greek and the Hindu by wisdom knew not God. They knew philosophy about God, not God. Just as I had finished that sentence a note came from a Hindu friend commenting on the Round Table held to-day: "Another point which I could not but notice was the absence of even a single statement of experience on the part of some of us who inhabit this Eastern world and who ever speak of religion as though it were religion alone that permeates us all the twenty-four hours of the day and night, while those of the Christians were, to my mind, to say the least, superb. You had found."

Both the Greek and the Hindu were impatient of the moral and wanted to go directly to the light. Religion among the Greeks and among the Hindus lacks moral basis. Someone has called our attention to the fact that there is not a villain in the Iliad—there wasn't a sufficiently developed moral sense to create a villain, as moral distinctions did not matter. In Hinduism philosophy has failed to appeal to the will. In the highest Brahma there is sat, chit, ananda— being, intelligence and bliss, but note there is no *will*. The highest Brahma is actionless. This lack of emphasis on the will has been responsible for the fact that religion in India has failed to regenerate life and to cleanse society, for it has been impatient of the moral, has tried to vault over it and to get to light without righteousness. But as the candle that illuminates burns out of the definite physical basis of wick and wax, so the spiritual life that illuminates burns out of the definite basis of right moral living in right human relationships. You may cry for light without physical bulb, or wax or wood, as they seem to be too earthy, but a light without a phys- ical basis is a will-o'-the-wisp. A lantern is an humble thing, but it lights us home while the floating will-o'-the-wisp leaves us finally in the dark—and often in the bog. Jesus was right when he said, "Salvation is of the Jews," for they insisted that religion first of all meant righteous- ness or nothing.

But if salvation is of the Jews, it does not stop there. The Jew needs the Greek—and also the Hindu. The Jew was not sufficiently compre- hensive. He was definite, not infinite. The Jew- ish religion has the candlestick as its symbol. There was too much candlestick and not enough of broad-shining and pervading light. Religion among the Semites was not symmetrical. It was often narrow, fanatical, ready to exterminate its enemies and to believe the extermination to be by divine sanction. Islam is Semitic to the core, hence fanatical and exclusive. Christianity too has not yet sloughed off completely the chrysalis out of which it emerged. It must slough it off or be crippled. If the gospel had stayed only among the Jews, it would have died, pot-bound. The assimilating of the Greek idea of the Word was the most important development that theology ever took, said Harnack. It gave Christ a cosmic setting. So too the gospel coming into contact with the comprehensive Hindu mind is giving us larger categories for our thought of Christ and his gospel. The missionary in going to another nation unconsciously becomes a missionary to his own people. He brings back larger categories in which to interpret Christ. Paul did. John did. The modern missionary does. And we have wider conceptions of Christ as a result. The Lushais of the Assam hills have a name for foreigner which means, "he who spoils us." Jesus gives us a conception of the foreigner which might be defined as "he who may enrich us." Of the twain, Jew and Gentile, said Paul, we are going to make a new man, and he might have added—a bigger one!

In Jesus Christ we are to be the salt of the Hebrew and the light of the Greek—and more!

CHAPTER VII

WHAT CHRIST AND THEY ARE
TO THE FUTURE

THE idea of fulfillment in the Gospels is distinctive and of great value in producing right attitudes toward other faiths and cultures. It was a great day in Christian missions in India when we turned the corner from the former iconoclastic, unappreciative attitudes to those of appreciation, of gathering up every vital truth and beauty in the past. The pivot on which this change took place was the idea of fulfillment. I was with some students at Hardwar, where the sacred Ganges issues from the Himalayas into the plains. As we were getting into a boat to go across, some of the students thoughtlessly began to throw stones into the Ganges. A kindly-faced old sannyasi said in a grieved tone: "You throw stones into Mother Ganges, but I throw flowers," and he then proceeded to strew flowers upon the sacred waters.

"Give me some of the flowers," I said, "I too wish to throw them into the Ganges, not, of course, with your meaning, but still I'll throw them in as a symbol of my reverence for India."

He acknowledged the difference between our casting of the flowers, but was deeply grateful that I took that attitude rather than that of throwing stones. For many decades Christian missions threw stones into the soul of India by controversy, by contempt of all that India held sacred and dear. India's sensitive soul writhed within her. And then the change took place. We began reverently to search India's religions and culture to find whatever of goodness, truth, and beauty we could find. Instead of stones we dropped flowers of appreciation and gratitude. We could urge with deep sincerity that India keep her own soul, that only thus could she be creative instead of being merely copyist. When I first came to India, I did not want to find anything good in India, lest if I did there should be no place for my gospel. However, I was uneasy within. I felt there was something wrong. When I got hold of this idea of fulfillment in its full meaning, I sighed a sigh of relief. I could be the friend and lover of India and still hold to my gospel.

This attitude is good up to a certain point. After that it may become maudlin sentimentality, even as ripeness beyond a certain point turns into rottenness. The idea of fulfillment with its attitudes of appreciation is now on the verge, in many places, of passing into a mushy sentimentality in which the love of truth is submerged and drowned.

It is important that Jesus, after announcing that he came not to destroy but to fulfill, now passes on and says to his disciples that this idea of fulfillment did not mean that they should stop at the past and not go on beyond it—"Except your righteousness shall exceed the righteousness of the scribes and the Pharisees"—the best representatives of the past—you shall not enter this new kingdom. He says that what he was bringing was not the sum total of the past, much less a mere echo of it. They must go beyond the old or not get into the new. The gospel is religion plus.

We have not always paid attention to this plus attitude demanded of us. In fact, much of our righteousness, collective and personal, does not exceed the righteousness of the old. A responsible Christian journal which prides itself on its adherence to the gospel cites the Old Testament wars of extermination as a proof that war is legitimate for a Christian. When the writer of the psalm prays that the children of his enemies might be dashed to pieces upon a rock I, as a Christian, cannot pray that prayer and remain Christian. I must go beyond that spirit or not enter that kingdom of love in which we love our enemies and do good to them that despitefully use us. Many of us fulfill the Ten Commandments and think that we are thereby Christians. But Jesus says, "A new commandment I give unto you, that you love one another, even as I have loved you"—and that exceeds, far exceeds, the righteousness of the Ten Commandments. A village worker lined up his people in the village to show me how much his people knew about Christianity. He asked them what happened on the first day of creation, on the second day, and so on, and when they answered triumphantly he turned to me and said, "They know a lot about Christianity, don't they?" I asked him if knowing what happened on the first day or the third day would save anybody? We smile at the village worker, and yet many sections of Christendom have never gotten beyond the ethics and the spirit of the Old Testament to the New. We are pre-Christian. The Crusaders sang, "Fairest Lord Jesus, ruler of all nature," and then in his gentle name waded through blood in the streets of Jerusalem and praised him as they dashed out the brains of little children. Jesus was the ruler of all nature, but certainly not of their natures. Sir John Bowring sits on a slave ship and writes the hymn: "In the Cross of Christ I Glory," while beneath him the hold of the ship was filled with manacled and wretched slaves. As Christ sat manacled and tortured with them he could not hear the hymn of praise, for his ears and his heart were filled with the groans of his brethren about him. When the lathi blows were falling on the unresisting heads of the satyagrahas in the streets of Bombay, a bishop when asked why in the name of Christ and humanity he did not protest, replied, "Men will never learn anything except through blows," and then probably turned to the hymning of the Crucified, who learned through blows to be the Saviour of even the bishop.

You must go beyond the old or fail to get into the new. Your righteousness must exceed the righteousness of the Pharisee and the scribe, which was a legal righteousness. Yours must be a love righteousness; your righteousness must exceed that of the Hindu ascetic, for he strives for personal deliverance and you must strive for the kingdom of heaven on earth; your righteousness must exceed that of the Buddhist, for at the heart of his righteousness is a bitter disillusionment and at the heart of yours must be an Easter morning; your righteousness must exceed that of the Moslem, for his righteousness is a slave righteousness and yours must be that of a free man; your righteousness must exceed that of the Confucianist, for he strives to be a superior man and you must strive to be the servant of all; your righteousness must exceed that of the delicately calculating moralist, for yours is a righteousness that does not calculate—it is that of the second mile and of the other cheek; your righteousness must exceed that of the half-Christian who is content with the mind of Moses instead of going on to the mind of the Master.

The gospel is not the echo of Sinai, but the voice of Calvary. It is not the priest-of-things-as-they-are, but the prophet-of-things-as-they ought-to-be. You remember Jesus had said to his disciples that "so persecuted they the prophets which were before you." The prophets which were before you—you are in the line of prophetic succession, you are the spirit of the years to come mingling itself with the present. There is a difference between Moses and Jesus. Moses stood on the mount and viewed the Promised Land, Jesus sat on the mount and revealed the Promised Humanity; Moses viewed the Promised Land but did not enter; Jesus was the Promised Humanity, its illustration and its goal. Moses gave a set of new commands; Jesus gave the set of the new character.

The set of the new character is different from the mind-set of ordinary humanity. It is character that is motivated by love, that is ministering by self-sacrifice, and that is moving on toward Christlikeness. Islam boasts that it accommodates itself to human nature. The gospel glories in the fact that it accommodates human nature by regeneration to the ideal of perfection. This character is bound to "exceed," for the goal set before it exceeds anything ever set up.

Jesus does not stop here. He had indeed announced the doctrine of fulfillment, but he now goes on and puts his finger on the places where the past is wrong and where it fails, and takes the astonishing attitude that his own word is authoritative and final by saying, "But I say unto you." The doctrine of fulfillment is followed by that of his own final authoritativeness. This is of the utmost importance, for without this the idea of fulfillment tends to end up in a syncretism.

One of the greatest dangers to the Christian movement in the East is the danger of syncretism. At the top there is a fading out of any clear-cut issue between Christ and other ways of life. The tendency is to put flowers gathered from many places into a religious bouquet. The bouquet may be beautiful, but since it has no roots of its own, it withers and dies. Syncretism in philosophy belongs to that period when philosophy has ceased to be creative and can only gather up what has been created. This is also true of syncretism in religion. It seems to be a sign of broadness. It is really a sign of decay. Glover tells us that, among the ancients "Poseidonius was the arch-reconciler, the arch-eclectic, and it is of interest to note at once how wide was his influence and how short-lived and how utterly his books have perished." Novalis says, "All eclectics are essentially and at bottom skeptics, the more comprehensive the more skeptical." The Brahmo Samaj is a theistic eclecticism and has given full rein to this syncretic tendency. We would have thought that through its liberalism and its fine-spiritedness it would have swept the country. But the result? Listen to what one of its ministers said to me:

"I stopped preaching because I had nothing

to preach. I had no message. I went to Calcutta and found the movement drying up at its center. It has no dynamic. It is a mere collection of beautiful things."

This is what will and does happen to the Christian movement when it stops at fulfillment; or when, as in Unitarianism, it lacks the authority of a Divine "But I say unto you." It is the "But I say unto you" that gives it moral and spiritual authority and evangelistic dynamic. The difficulty with the doctrine of fulfillment is that it tends to stop there and make Jesus the sum total of beautiful things. This ends in a paralysis and an impasse. But he is more. He is the Plus. It is the Plus in Jesus that gives moral authority and that saves us. The Brahmo Samaj has no Plus. It has the many, but not the Other. It is this failure to go on to the Plus that paralyzes so many liberal minds. They proclaim truths but not the Truth. They are syncretic but not evangelistic. They announce news, but not the Good News. They teach as the scribes, who echo the past, and not as the Christ who assumes control over the present and the future.

It is no secret that the Christian movement in the East is at the parting of the ways. We cannot go back to the old unsympathetic, iconoclastic attitudes of the past, but if, on the other hand, we yield to the tendencies of the hour both from within the movement itself and from the

sympathetic Hindu, then we shall be like the
river in Africa that starts toward the sea, but
gets lost in the sand and disappears. The genius of Hinduism is its all-inclusiveness. Many of
our Hindu friends would like that all-inclusiveness to include Christ and his gospel and leave
it at that. It is the "But I say unto you" of final
authority that is the rock of stumbling. There
is the Christ of "I came not to destroy but to
fulfill," of agreement, of fulfillment, but there is
also the Christ of "But I say unto you," of dis-
agreement, of challenge, of change, of final
authority. India is ready to accept the Christ
of fulfillment—we all are; but it is because of
this Christ of change, of going beyond, of ultimate demand, who is so imperious, that we often
go back and walk no more with him. Just there
is the crux of the battle of the future. And the
issue is this: whether in Christ we hear merely
beautiful words or whether we hear God's saving word.

For it is this Plus that saves us. There are
two things in Jesus—one like me, and one unlike
me. He meets life as a man, calls on no power
that is not at your disposal and mine. He is so
like me that I feel I might put my hand on his
shoulder and say, "Brother man." But the moment I am about to do it I am confronted with
that something in him that is unlike me. He
confronts me with an offer of salvation that only
God can offer. So instead of putting my hand

on his shoulder, I find myself at his feet. It is this unlikeness to me that saves me. We need both the likeness and the unlikeness. He is like me, therefore my Example; he is unlike me, therefore my Redeemer. If he were only like me, he could not be my Redeemer; if he were only unlike me, he could not be my Example. It is the combination of the likeness and the unlikeness that gives me what I need.

In the larger sense, as between systems, we find Christ like others in that he fulfills their finest; but he is unlike them in that he says—"But I say unto you." And unless we can retain the authority of that Plus we have an Example, but no Redeemer.

We must get hold of the importance of this statement, for it is true that: "The differences are the vitalities of a religion." Professor Radhakrishan, one of the greatest of modern exponents of the all-inclusiveness of Hinduism, acknowledged that the above statement was true and named "the realization of the spiritual" as the distinctive contribution of Hinduism.

What is it in Christianity that makes it different and therefore gives it vitality? Obviously it is not a particular doctrine or teaching, for many other religions have similar teachings. It is this Person, who, standing amid ancient codes and ways of life, dares say: "But I say unto you." The uniqueness of Jesus lies in his total personality. "We have everything in the Gita that you

have," said a Hindu to me one day. "Yes," I
replied, "everything except Christ." He himself
is the difference in the gospel that gives it a
mighty vitality. The gospel lies in his Person—
he himself is the Good News.

Jesus announced himself as the light of the
world. Light is made up of the sum total of
the colors of the spectrum. Jesus as light gathers up the different colored truths and goodness
of all who have gone before. Each one can find
his distinctive national or religious color in
Christ. But we do not want colors—we want
light. Christ is the sum-total of the colors, but
he is more. He is light itself. A Bahaist lady
came from the West and speaking to an Indian
audience in Gujarat with a Parsee gentleman as
an interpreter. She said to the audience that
when the sun arose, it arose in the East and
shone through window after window in the
house. Each window represented a religion and
each window thought that it had the light. Jesus
was a window and Buddha was a window, but
there was One Sun shining through them all.
The Parsee interpreter added this to his interpretation: "I beg to differ from the lady. Jesus
is not just a window. He is the Sun shining
into these other windows. He is light itself."

It was a moment of very tense silence when,
at the Jerusalem Conference, Professor Otto
said to us: "I went out to India with the idea
that Christ was the prolongation of other truths,

but not essentially different. I have come back convinced that in Christ we have not merely a prolongation of other truths, but the difference in quantity is so great that it amounts to a difference in quality. He is not merely the More—He is the Other." It is this Other that brings me to his feet and will, I believe, bring the world to his feet.

Jesus gives the proper order in first saying that he had come to gather up everything that is beautiful in the past and then in going on to put his finger on the places where that past fails. You cannot overthrow a wrong or error unless you first recognize the truth that is hidden away in that wrong or error and which makes it live. After acknowledging the truth that may be there you are then in a position to hit and to hit hard the error or the wrong. In coming to the East we reversed the process. We were first iconoclastic, unsympathetic, and pugnacious. We ridiculed the beliefs and customs of the people, so that the sensitive soul of the East closed up. Then we turned and began to talk of the beauties in the heritage of India and that we had not come to destroy but to fulfill them. But the mischief had been done. A heritage of wounded susceptibilities and hence suspicion meets us. Had we done as Jesus did, talked of fulfillment first and then gone on to loving criticism, India would have had a heart to listen. In our imperiousness and in our cocksureness we missed step with our Master. We are now trying to regain it.

We have had three methods of evangelism: Destructive Criticism, Constructive Fulfillment, and the Direct Method. By the Direct Method I mean the direct presentation of Christ as the fulfillment of the past and yet as the More, the Plus, the Other that saves us.

Fulfillment? Yes, but also the facing of facts. Constructive? Yes, and in that very constructiveness, critical. Someone has said that: "The systems that are less complete lead of necessity to the systems that are more complete. The method is constructive and reconstructive. It is critical as the blossom is critical of the bud, and as the bud of the thorn on which it grew. There is a genetic movement in life. As higher forms recapitulate lower forms so there is a kindred movement in thought upon the things of life, but neither is subversive, each is reconstructive. And being reconstructive it is critical." Jesus would fulfill—yes. But as he did for the Hebrew so he would do for the Hindu: "Ye have heard it said of old time by the writer of the Gita that war is legitimate and right and according to dharma, but I say unto you that war is sin, and that they that take the sword shall perish with the sword." Again, "Ye have heard it said of old time that God in the highest form is an impersonal It, but I say unto you that the Father is love, and, being love, he cannot be the Impersonal." Again, "Ye have heard it said of old time that the world is not worth changing; escape it; but I say unto you that ye pray and work that the kingdom of God may come on earth, for it is my desire that you should not be taken out of the world but that ye should be kept from the evil one." Again, "Ye have heard it said of old time that God is like the images that are by the wayside, but I say unto you that he is not—He that hath seen me hath seen the Father." No namby-pamby talk of the equal worth of all religious ideas in Christ. He is tender, but truthful; sympathetic, but severe.

Again and again people say to me that all religions are equally good; that as all rivers run into the ocean, so all religions go to the same goal. My reply is that it is not true that all rivers run into the ocean—the Jordan River runs into the Dead Sea and stays there, and many earnest ways of life run into Dead Seas of futility. If you will not let me pick and choose my values in religion, then I am sorry, but I am through with all religions, for I see that religion has not always been a blessing to humanity. In Jesus there is no maudlin sentimentality. There is sympathy combined with realism. This attitude of his lays deep hold upon my heart.

If the plant of the gospel does put its roots into the soil of India and gather out all that is akin to its own nature and takes it up into itself, nevertheless it rejects as well as selects. Life depends upon elimination as well as upon assimilation. I love the Christ of "I came not to destroy," but I love more the Christ of "But I say unto you." The first Christ saves truths, the second Christ saves me.

THE NEW MORALS—BASED ON
REVERENCE FOR PERSONALITY

CHAPTER VIII

REVERENCE FOR THE PERSONALITIES OF THE SOCIALLY INFERIOR

JESUS now tests the old in the light of a searching test—reverence for personality. He brings everything to the bar of the question, What does it think of, and how does it treat a person? His new righteousness that exceeds is based on reverence for personality. To him there was nothing sacred save personality—neither vessels, nor rites, nor ceremonies, nor places. If any of these were sacred at all, they were sacred only derivatively as associated with the only intrinsically sacred thing—personality. Note the groups for which he demands reverence of personality.

1. Reverence for those who are in a class below us (verses 21-22). (Usually we do not speak contemptuously to those who are on our own so-called social level, to those who have a comeback.)

2. Reverence for those on the same social level (verses 23-26).

(*a*) Our brother who has aught against us.

(*b*) Our adversary who is able to go to law with us.

3. Reverence for the personality of woman (verses 27-28).

4. Reverence for our own personality (verses 29-30).

5. Reverence for truth in speech, or, better still, for every man with whom we speak, so much so that we will not mislead him by overstatement or exaggeration (verses 33-37).

6. Reverence for the personalities of those who are in a so-called class above us—those who can flick our cheeks, and can compel us to go a mile (verses 39-41).

7. Reverence for the personalities of those who are economically beneath us (verse 42).

8. Reverence for our enemies (verses 43-47).

Reverence for personality is the basis of Jesus' teaching in regard to our duties to man. It is quite true, as Glover has said, that Jesus did not use words ending in "ity," which we are so fond of using. He did not talk of personality, he talked of persons. He did not ask us to love humanity, he asked us to love people. It costs little to enthuse about love of humanity, for it is so vague and abstract that it demands nothing but sentiment. Someone is reported to have said, "I love humanity, but I don't like people." And it was said of Rousseau that "he combined love of all mankind in general with hatred of all mankind in particular." "Isn't love of humanity a purer form of love than love for persons, since the latter may have other elements in it?" asked a rather sentimental lady of me. I replied that it might be so pure as to be pure abstraction. While recognizing this tendency to abstraction, however, we will use the term "personality," but we will try to put within it the flesh-and-blood content that Jesus would put there.

Jesus brought not only a revelation of God—he brought a revelation of man. Simeon said that Jesus would be "a light to unveil (marg.) the Gentiles." He would unveil the possibilities that lie in all human personality, even in that of the "Gentile dogs." He believed that all men were of infinite worth apart from race and birth and color and money and social standing. There are seven sayings of Jesus that are the most formative utterances ever spoken in religion in reference to the emancipation of man. They are: (1) The Sabbath was made for man and not man for the Sabbath. (2) When you bring your gift to God and there remember that your brother has anything against you in the nature of personal, social, economic, or political injustice or misunderstanding, go, be reconciled and then come and offer the gift. (3) Go learn what this means—I desire mercy between man and man and not sacrifice. (4) That which goeth into the man does not defile him, but that which comes out defiles him—this he said making all meats clean. (5) Do unto others as ye would that men should do unto you. (6) Thou shalt love thy neighbor as thyself. (7) A new commandment I give you, That ye love one another as I have loved you.

These are the seven colors that blend themselves into the white light that is now beating on all human institutions and all human relationships. You can no more get rid of them and live humanly than you can get rid of light and live physically. Take but one of them—the Sabbath was made for man and not man for the Sabbath. All rites, all ceremonies, all religious institutions, all social organizations, all political states—all are made for man and not man for them, and they must be judged by one question: What do they do to, and for, the personality of man? Never was uttered anything more revolutionary than this. There is enough dynamite in that simple statement to blow many of our existing institutions to pieces, for they cannot stand this human test. I once saw some men with hooks stuck through the flesh of their backs drawing an idol car through the streets of a city by ropes attached to these hooks. Religion pulled along at the expense of the torn bodies of men! Many of our institutions are being dragged along by the lacerated bodies and minds and souls of men. Men are made for them, they are not made for men. If we had eyes to see, we could see the gilded cars of many of the idle rich pulled along by the hooks stuck in the backs of the exploited factory operatives—men, women, and little children.

Jesus saw the leaders of Jerusalem allow the Temple, which was to be a house of prayer for all nations, gradually become the embodiment of a contempt for personality. Into the place where the Gentiles were allowed they put sheep and cattle and money-changing—things taking the place of men, and a racial snobbery at the heart of it all. It was the profanation of personality, not the profanation of the Temple that made him cleanse it. The scourge of Christ is to-day upon the back of any system—be it religious or otherwise, that stands for things against men and that has a contempt for men at the heart of it.

Jesus had a passion for man. Talking with a Hindu doctor who had performed a hundred thousand operations on the eye, I asked him what the secret of it was. He thought a moment and then answered, "I was mad after eyes." Beautiful passion! Jesus was mad after men. When General Booth stood before Queen Victoria and was asked what she might do for him, the rugged saint replied: "Your Majesty, some people's passion is money, and some people's passion is fame, but my passion has been men." In this he echoed the mind of his Master.

Jesus now turns in his Sermon from world-encompassing and system-encompassing terms to the individual. He did not lose sight of the individual man in talking about "the world" and "the earth." The bishops of the Methodist Episcopal Church were assembled when the news reached them of the signing of the armistice after the Great War. Everyone was delirious

with joy. They called on Bishop Quayle to give
a speech. They expected him in his eloquent and
inimitable way to laud the victory of the Allies
and the glories of the peace. Instead he arose
and amazed them all by pleading that now they
give just and brotherly treatment to the Negro.
No victory for him that did not mean a victory
for the unprivileged. So Jesus turns here to
the man.

He says: "Ye have heard that it was said to
them of old time, That thou shalt not kill; and
whosoever shall kill shall be in danger of the
judgment; but I say unto you, that everyone
who is angry with his brother shall be in danger
of the judgment; and whosoever shall say to his
brother, Raca, shall be in danger of the council;
and whosoever shall say, Thou fool, shall be in
danger of the hell of fire" (verses 21-23). Here
anger with the brother is equal to murder; contemptuous phrases toward him are equal to
blasphemy; assumption of the right to dispense
condemnation to him is equal to the sin with the
severest penalties attached—these verses are a
burning declaration of human worth. Note that
"without a cause" has been dropped out in the
Revised Version, thereby canceling the attempt
to de-Christianize the verse by toning it down.
Thou shalt not murder the body of another, said
the Old; Thou shalt not murder the soul of
another by contempt, said Jesus. Thou shalt not
blaspheme God, said the Old; Thou shalt not

blaspheme man, for to blaspheme him is to blaspheme God, said Jesus. Any phrase, any attitude, any look that lowers a man's self-respect, that degrades him in his own eyes, is soul-murder, said Jesus. To him the sin of sins was contempt.

He that says to his Eastern brother, "Native," "Chinaman," "Jap," shall be in danger of the council of collective opinion, a growing moral sentiment; and if he goes too far, he will find himself in the fires of rebellion. He that says to his brother "Nigger," shall be in danger of the council of growing collective judgment, and he who says, "Thou fool," shall be in danger of the hell of fire of seeing the Negro surpass him in intellectual and moral character. "Thou fool" comes back with terrific and terrifying force. You murder the soul of another and the ghost of his spirit haunts your councils, your national legislatures, and your very national life. In Brazil I came in contact with the remnants of some people who left the Southern states after the Civil War rather than stay in a land where the Negro was free. The Nemesis was that they went into a land where the Negroes, slaves then, but now free, have come into the largest social freedom and equality with the white man of any place in the world! These emigrants deteriorated. They lived on a prejudice and died of jaundice. The Anglo-Indian has said "Native" to the Indian, and the collective judgment of the

Indian people has segregated him and has left him in the hell of uncertainty as to where his future is to be. The Mestizo—the same class in the Philippines—has said to the Filipino, "My brother," and has found himself in leadership in that land. Agree, and you will find yourself in an agreeable world; refuse, and you will find yourself in a hell of isolation—damned by your own judgments.

Contempt has brought the white man to the judgment in India. "A change of heart" is what India demands in him. Thank God there are signs of that change of heart, and that is the only hope for the future. Depend upon it, the greatest fear is not "the rising tide of color," but the fear that there will not be a receding tide of color prejudice.

"Brahmanism has had its day," said an old Brahman to me. It has. It is dying of contempt. Everything else will die that has contempt at its heart. Contempt for classes who are supposed to be beneath us keeps us from sympathy for man as man. We can feel pain, provided it is the pain of our class or group. Outside that it seldom touches us. I once overheard the conversation of two English ladies concerning a British sergeant who was standing out in the pouring rain keeping back the people.

"Look at that poor sergeant, he is getting soaked," said one.

"But, he is only a sergeant," replied the other.

In her opinion a sergeant could not get wet, a commissioned officer would have been terribly wet! Then I heard her go on and talk about the snobbery of some people, evidently in a class above, toward her. And they were both indignant at it. Snobbery is from above to us below, not from us to the one below! We feel class-injustice and class-pain, not human pain.

"I am going to get off this ship, for there are nothing but working people on it," I overheard an English lady say in high dudgeon. A few swift months went by and those same "working people" were in charge of and running the Ship of State, and she had not only to be on the same ship with them, but had to obey their commands. And unless she has had a change of heart she is burning in the fires of her own contempt.

Jesus has been called "the great believer in man." The common people heard him gladly because he did not treat them as common people. Three words were constantly upon his lips: the least, the last, and the lost. These words were upon his lips for these people were in his heart. I once saw in a temple a picture of the god Bhagwan bending over the prostrate form of a man and tearing open his entrails with his finger nails. "It shows his power," remarked the priest. I see in the pages of the New Testament a picture of Christ bending over the prostrate form of man and with infinite tenderness healing every hurt of soul and body. "It shows his loving power," we whisper to one another, our hearts reverent and gripped to their very depths. It is no wonder that contempt was to him equal to blasphemy.

He goes on and enforces this by saying: "If therefore thou art offering thy gift at the altar, and there rememberest that thy brother hath aught against thee, leave there thy gift before the altar, and go thy way, first be reconciled to thy brother, and then come and offer thy gift" (verses 23-24). Here religion and right human relationships are indissolubly linked together. Anything that shuts out my brother shuts out God. "Leave there thy gift before the altar"—not on it, God will consider it blasphemy if you come before him unreconciled to your brother. Never were religion and the highest humanism so made one as here. Hold up all worship, Jesus said, until you hold your brother in your heart in love and reverence. This verse would render unchristian a vast amount of Christianity.

The Christians of the United States, knowing that the Negro has aught against them, should leave their gift before the altar and go and be reconciled with their Negro brother in a thoroughgoing reconciliation and then come and offer their gift. The British Christians, knowing that India has aught against them, should leave their gift and be reconciled with their Indian brothers in a reconciliation that would mean utter equality of status and opportunity and then come and offer their gift. The Brahmans of India should cease praying and go and be reconciled and do prayaschit (repentance) for the wrongs done to the outcastes and come and offer their gifts or else be prepared to pay the utmost farthing of being ousted. The Hindu, hurt and lashing back at the snobbishness of the Westerner, but himself infected with a caste snobbery that would exclude the Westerner from his home, must go and be reconciled or be strangled by his own narrowness. Capitalism, knowing that Labor has aught against it for its exploitation, should go and be reconciled or else be prepared to pay the utmost farthing—the utmost farthing of being evicted by Bolshevism. The white races of the world, knowing that the colored races have aught against them for their snobbery and their exclusiveness and contempts, should go and be reconciled to their brother or else be prepared to pay the utmost farthing—a clash of color. The Protestant Churches, knowing that the "Catholic" bodies have aught against them for their dividing the Body of Christ into innumerable sects, should go and be reconciled with their brothers, or else be prepared to pay the utmost farthing of subdivision unto extinction. The Church of England and the High Churches in general, knowing that the Free Churches have aught against them for their snobbery and for the near-blasphemy of saying that the ministry of ministers used and accepted of God is not acceptable or valid to them, should leave off their prayers and be reconciled to their brothers or else pay the utmost farthing of being left "high"—and dry.

The acceptability of our giving to God is determined by our way of living with man. This lays on religion such a heavy moral obligation toward man that its very existence depends on its being able to discharge that moral obligation. This weight of moral obligation pressed so heavily on the Jewish ceremonial system of offering to God that it broke down. Men began to feel the futility of incense when what was needed was the aroma of humane deeds. The quickest way to break down an inadequate system is to lay on it a heavy moral obligation. Religion will not fail in the West because of skepticism or the growth of atheism. It will fail only if it fails in discharging the moral obligations in human relationships that modern life lays upon it. Much of Christianity in the West is breaking because it cannot meet this demand. Religion must discharge that obligation to society or else society will be obliged to discharge religion. Hinduism and Buddhism and Islam are breaking down in the East because of the growing moral demands being laid upon them. These religions have hitherto sheltered under the British government, and the weight of modern conditions has rested upon an outside government. Now that sheltered position is being taken away and the weight of the demand for modern progress is being laid straight upon these systems. It is cracking them. They must meet these moral demands for sustaining reforms in personal, social, economic, and political life or fail. They are failing, for religion of that type stands for yesterday, not for to-day and to-morrow. They are not behind reforms—they are either indifferent to or blocking them. A Hindu judicial officer of Assam received an urgent wire to go to a flooded area and report on what measures of relief were necessary. He waited two days for a propitious day according to the stars and then went—too late. He was demoted by government. Religion waiting for a propitious day to help flood-stricken people! Religion that gazes at stars while human needs are crying to it for solution will find itself demoted by the collective judgment of mankind.

Religion that cannot discharge its moral and social obligations may be kept alive by means of artificial respiration, but not for long. I once saw a stuffy temple with a Western system of pumping air into it from the outside to make bearable the heat within. Religion may pump the outside air of reading scientific meanings into unscientific systems, making them modern by the process of spiritualization, and try to keep them alive by smuggling the outside air of imported ideas into them, but it is all useless,

for religion will only live as it can genuinely
meet by its own inherent vitality and moral
power the moral demands made upon it. In one
place in India 1336 priests sat and chanted sacred verses for two weeks in order to ward off
the growing menace of modern progress to religion. Religion repeating verses will not ward
off these dangers either in East or West, they
can only be met by giving something to human
life that nothing else can give.

In verses 25, 26 Jesus goes on and further emphasizes this demand for reverence for personality by insisting that you agree with your adversary quickly while you are in the way, before
the processes of law set in. You must settle it,
not by the processes of law, but by the power
of love. If you go in for legal processes, then
legal processes will get you, and you will pay
the utmost farthing. You will either begin with
humility or end with humiliation. The Christian is under obligation to settle a misunderstanding whether the brother has aught against
him as in verse 24, or whether he is the one
who has wronged another as in Matthew 18. 15.
In either case, wronged or having wronged, the
Christian must go to all lengths to settle. Forgiveness of injuries, Seeley says, is the distinctive Christian spirit. He is right. Do not let
bitterness stay for a single moment lest it poison
the whole springs of life, says Jesus. A village
woman with a very bad abscess came to a doctor

in India. She pleaded for a plaster to put over it instead of opening it with the knife as the doctor suggested. He insisted that he must get out the poison lest it spread to her heart and kill her. She begged for the plaster, refused the knife, and went home. As predicted, the poison spread to her heart and killed her. Jesus insists that we do not cover up with the plasters of self-justification and self-excuse these misunderstandings and hatreds, lest they poison our inmost souls and kill us spiritually.

To sum up: Reverence for the personalities of those with whom you dare be contemptuous, since they are beneath you socially and hence have no come-back; of those who are on the same social level, brothers, but who have been wronged by you; of those who are your adversaries in law. In short, reverence for personality is the foundation of the New Humanity. But it is more than reverence for personality; rather it is a loving reverence for personality. It is this "enthusiasm for humanity" which lies at the heart of the gospel that makes it live in a world of human demands. Jesus believed in people, hence people believed in Jesus. As Chesterton said of Saint Francis: "The secret of his success was his profound belief in other people. . . . He used to talk to thieves and robbers about their misfortune of not being able to give vent to their desire for holiness." In this Saint Francis was true to the mind of his Master.

CHAPTER IX

REVERENCE FOR THE PERSONALITY OF WOMAN

JESUS now turns, in discussing the sex question, to reverence for the personality of woman (chapter 5, verses 27, 28, 31-33), and reverence for one's own personality (verses 29, 30).

The aseptic quality of Jesus' mind can be seen nowhere else in such crystal clearness as in his dealing with sex. But it was aseptic, not ascetic. Unmarried himself, the only institution he ever defended was the home, founding it, in contrast to the old Mosaic law, on the love of one man and one woman until death parted them. If the human race comes to monogamy—and it will, for it is the highest stage of sex relationship— then we must remember that it was the hand of the unmarried Galilæan that turned the switch, for up to his time polygamy was practically world-wide.

Jesus' attitude toward sex purity is in deep contrast with that of the best of the ancients on the one hand, and that of the modern attitudes on the other. Aristotle believed that woman was God's failure to make a man. Xenophon describes how "Socrates, having heard of the beauty of the courtesan Theodata, went with his disciples to ascertain for himself whether the report were true; how with quiet humor he questioned her about the sources of the luxury of her dwelling, and how he proceeded to sketch for her the qualities she should cultivate in order to attach her lovers to herself. Having carried on a cheerful and perfectly unembarrassed conversation with her, with no kind of reproach on his part and with no trace of the consciousness of guilt on hers, the best and wisest of the Greeks left his hostess with a graceful compliment to her beauty." No conscience about the gilded rottenness of it all. Modern thought too is loose, where looseness means disaster. Jesus set back the sin of adultery from the deed to the inner thought. A great deal of modern thought does not set it even at the place of the deed, but beyond the deed to the results of the deed. Modern ideas say, "Thou shalt not conceive"; Jesus says, "Thou shalt not conceive within thy heart the adulterous thought." And between these two there is a great gulf of impurity fixed.

Some outcastes in India were in Conference. A speaker from among them said: "We are the greatest of all peoples. When we get through with this life, three rivers confront us. One is a river of cow's blood—that turns back the Hindu; another is a river of swine's blood—that turns back the Mohammedan; and then there is a river of filth—that turns back the Christian. But we wade through all without hesitation and are therefore the greatest of all." The river of moral filth does turn back the Christian. His inner nature, partaking of the purity of Christ, revolts from it. But the sophisticated modern stops at nothing, wades through all, including the river of filth, and becomes one with the moral outcasts whose chief distinction is that nothing stains their already stained souls. A young man asked a Brahman tea-stall man for tea. The Brahman refused on the ground that he was low caste. "I am not, I am a Christian," he affirmed.

"No," said the Brahman, "you are not. You are not clean enough for a Christian."

The Brahman was right, for to be a Christian is to be clean in body and soul.

Jesus stands for reverence for the personality of the woman. In one place it is said of Jesus, "He laid his hands upon her: and immediately she was made straight." When the hands of a good deal of modern teaching are laid on woman, immediately she is made crooked. Jesus insisted that she must not be a means to man's ends, but that she is an end in herself, and must be treated as such. Looking on her as a sex-being and that alone is adulterous thinking. The whole of the purdah idea, while ostensibly to protect the purity of the woman, looks on woman only as a creature of sex, and is therefore essentially adulterous in its thinking. The holiest among the Pharisees were called "the bleeding Pharisees." They went around with their eyes on the ground, lest they look on a woman, and as they were constantly bumping against trees and posts and walls, they had bleeding foreheads—hence holy. How sane and yet how severe Jesus was! He lifted up men's eyes to look frankly at life, but in that freedom there was the restraint of an inner purity.

Jesus says, "Thou shalt not think adultery." He emphasizes what has become plain to the psychologists, namely, that ideas are motor; that if you hold them within the mind by their very presence there they will pass straight into act. If you hold them in the mind long enough, they will brush past your will and become action in spite of all your protests. The statement many times repeated cannot be repeated too often: Sow a thought and you reap an act, sow an act and you reap a habit, sow a habit and you reap a character, sow a character and you reap a destiny. Note that the thought has to be sown, it will bring forth no act if it is dismissed at once. The sin is not in the coming of the thought, it is in the holding of it, the harboring of it. Thoughts of sin become sinful thoughts only when they are held and harbored. "You cannot help the birds flying over your heads, but you can help them building nests in your hair"— you cannot help the vagrant thoughts flying through your mind, but you can help brooding over them, warming them, and thus hatching them into action. "I look only at the best pictures," said the great painter Sir Joshua Reynolds, "for the bad ones spoil my eyes."

Be careful that there is no sag at the place of sex-thought, said Jesus, for if you let down here, then the whole of life will sag with it. The battle of life as a whole cannot rise higher than the sexual battle. Lose here and you lose all down the battleline of life. Jesus insists on drastic treatments. He says that if thy right eye, or thy right hand, or thy foot causeth thee to stumble, cut it off or pluck it out and cast it from thee (verses 29, 30). If thy right hand offend thee—suppress on the lower that you may express on the higher. Here is the principle for self-expression: Express every legitimate natural desire so long as it does not interfere with expression on the level of the higher nature. But the moment it does so interfere with, or lower the tone of the higher in the slightest, then give it up, or, in more modern jargon, cut it out! If the eye—the organ that sees; the hand—the organ that works; the foot—the organ that gives locomotion—from the highly organized and the dearest to the most ordinary, if anywhere there is stumbling—not falling, but stumbling—if it upsets you the slightest, makes you limp on your way to the goal of perfection, then cut it off. It is better to be maimed on the lower than on the higher. "For what is a man profited," said Jesus, "if he gain the whole world and lose or receive damage to his own soul or self?"

(Field's translation of Luke 8. 36). If in gaining the whole world of physical thrill the soul is damaged—not damned, but damaged—if it puts the soul off color in the least, then it is not worth it.

Many talk of self-expression when in reality they mean sex expression, or physical expression. But by the very expression of the physical the self, the real person, is suppressed. Then there is no self-expression, but self-stultification. I have watched the white ants come out of the ground during the rains. If it is night, they fly straight for the lamp, lose their wings, leaving a pile of them around the base of the lamp, and then crawl back into the earth again. That is the history of a good many people who experiment with sex. A brief flutter out of the earth, an attraction by the fire of sex, the loss of wings, and then the life lived underground again—in the dark. Herein is the difference between Jesus and modern thought: he was decisive in the matter of trifling with sex; modern thought is loose. Many have swung from Puritanism to impuritanism. But the future of the race belongs to the continent. Any race or group can rule that will subordinate a present desire for a larger goal. Any person who can say "No" on one level in order to be able to say "Yes" on a higher level emerges as a superior type. For sex cravings can be sublimated into higher forms of creative art, of poetry, of altruism, of service.

Subordination in order to sublimation should be the Christian attitude.

"But it is all right if you can get away with it," said a very ultra-modern young woman in my hearing. "If you can get away with it"— that's just the point. You cannot "get away with it," for it registers itself in inner deterioration, in the inner hell of not being able to respect yourself, in compelling you to live underground in blind labyrinths. You cannot "get away with it" either within or without. In the lines of Leighton:

"We cannot sway
  From truth and virtue but it draws a screen
  Over the face of day.
The flowers shut up their wonders from our eyes,
  Their beauty which enchanted us; and books
  Refuse to give their deeper sense that lies
  Revealed to virtuous looks.
To perfect purity—if such could be—
  The earth were all transparent—the dull clod
  In which we live nor beauty see—
  Breathing the living God."

The prodigal son found that when he went out to see life, he really saw death, for he cried out in his misery: "I have sinned against heaven [against the impersonal moral law], and in thy sight [against the personal love of the father]: and am no more worthy to be called thy son" [against himself]. When we sin we do not "get away with it"—we sin against Heaven—the impersonal moral law that breaks us if we break it; against the Father whose heart is broken by it; against ourselves, who in the end find ourselves broken—inwardly if not outwardly.

"If it offend, cut it off," are the decisive words of the purest Heart that ever beat. Note, however, that he does not say that it does necessarily offend. Herein is an essential difference between Christ and Buddhism and Hinduism. Hinduism says that the hand, the eye, and the foot do offend, for the physical is inherently evil—suppress it. Christ says that the physical members *may* offend, not that they necessarily do so, but that if they do, suppress them in order to a higher expression. One leads to asceticism pure and simple, the other to an asceticism only if the physical stands in the way. Hinduism teaches that the body is to be dismembered; the gospel teaches that the body is to be a member of Christ. He thereby makes the material a spiritual thing because dedicated to a spiritual purpose. "He is trying something that has not been attempted before, namely, to make not only his soul, but his body divine," said a French lady of Arabindo Ghose, the famous Indian mystic. But every sincere Christian who makes his members to be members of Christ does that very thing. "Your members" are to be "instruments of righteousness," says Paul. This is new. Hinduism would say that your members are always instruments of unrighteousness. They *may be,* says

the gospel, and in that case when the member becomes cancerous and spreads disease to the rest
of the being, cut it off!

To sum up: It is better that one of thy members perish than that thy whole body shall be cast
into hell—indulgence in sex may satisfy the sex
instinct, but what does it do to the rest of the
members, the rest of the personality? Does it
cast it into the hell of missing the mark, of in-
completeness—the hell of internal confusion re-
sulting from competing ends? Modern men seem
to look at sex alone and forget that the goal is
not the satisfaction of a particular passion, but
perfection, so that everything must be co-ordinated to that end.

. . . .

Jesus has been talking about reverence for the
personality of woman outside the marriage relation. He now turns toward reverence for her
personality inside the marriage relation. "It
was said also, Whosoever shall put away his
wife let him give her a writing of divorcement;
but I say unto you, that everyone that putteth
away his wife, saving for the cause of fornication,
maketh her an adulteress; and whosoever shall
marry her when she is put away commit-
teth adultery" (verses 31, 32). He says,
"Everyone that putteth away his wife . . .
maketh her an adulteress" in case she marries
again. This making of her an adulteress was a
greater sin than becoming an adulterer himself,

for it is a sin against the personality of another. And reverence for personality is the foundation of all morals with him.

The ancient Jew thought that his duty toward the woman was satisfied when he divorced her at will, but gave her a writing. No, said Jesus, it is not enough to give her a writing, you must give her yourself in indissoluble bonds—indissoluble except by death. The only thing that can dissolve the bond is death—physical death; or spiritual death—adultery. I take it that Matthew represents the mind of Christ when he added to Luke 16. 18, which makes no conditions whatever, the phrase "saving for the cause of fornication." I believe that the Roman Catholic practice is wrong in making no provision for divorce, and I believe that modern practice is wrong in going beyond the one provision Jesus made. Adultery by its very nature dissolves the bond, but nothing else does. Not at least for the Christian.

We must remember that Jesus was here speaking of marriage between disciples. Many of the marriages now performed in the Christian churches are not Christian in anything but name. Findlay rightly says: "It is exceedingly questionable whether we have any right to say in such cases 'Whom God has joined let no man put asunder,' and we should not seek to impose a law, meant to apply to Christian marriage, in a contract in which the only power that can make the marriage permanent has never, so far as we can tell, had a place." I believe with Findlay and Dean Inge that the only honest thing for the church to do is to refuse to perform marriages except between its own members, or at least between those who are prepared to make an open confession of faith, and then to insist that the marriage thus entered into should be indissoluble except by death.

For in case the marriage turns out badly the Christian has another alternative to divorce. He knows the secret of using pain and failure for higher ends. He can turn the incompatibilities in marriage to higher compatibilities with his Master. But the parties who are not Christian do not know that secret. In case of failure the divorce court is the only way open to them. Let them take it. But the door to the divorce court is not the only way open to the Christian; there is still open to him the door of using pain and of turning every impediment into an instrument and of using strained relationships as we use the tightening of the strings of a violin—to bring out finer music. As Walker well says: "Jesus opposed divorce because of the very fact that if it was a possibility, it acted as a culture to multiply the germs of discord in the family, whereas if people regarded it as a settled fact that they must put up with one another for the rest of their lives, they would do just what the oyster does when an irritating grain of sand has gotten in between its shells. They would put a pearl around it." Many a man or woman has climbed to sainthood over the rough path of incompatible marriage. Sour wives often make saintly husbands, and vice versa. This active dealing with the troubles and incompatibilities of married life, taking them up into one's higher purposes and making them contribute there, gives a new dimension to married life.

The alternatives for the Christian are not the nauseating idea of companionate marriage nor the equally nauseating idea of divorce; but should marriage turn out a failure—which seldom happens if both parties are determined it shall not be—then marriage failure may mean life success. The goal is perfection, and the hard blows of married life may serve only to chip off rough corners and make one more and more after that final image.

Jesus stood "in the treasury" which was in the Court of the women in the Temple and announced, "I am the light of the world." At the place of the two greatest problems of life, namely, money and women, Jesus said he was the light of the world. He is! Modern life missing his mind on these two things is plunging into deepening darkness, calling these deepening shadows "light."

CHAPTER X

REVERENCE FOR TRUTH

JESUS now emphasizes reverence for truth in the passage: "Again, ye have heard that it was said to them of old time, Thou shalt not forswear thyself, but shalt perform unto the Lord thine oaths: but I say unto you, Swear not at all, neither by the heaven, for it is the throne of God; nor by the earth, for it is the footstool of his feet; nor by Jerusalem, for it is the city of the great King. Neither shalt thou swear by thy head, for thou canst not make one hair white or black. But let your speech be Yea, yea; Nay, nay: and whatsoever is more than these is of the evil one" (chapter 5, verses 33-37).

The discussions on this passage usually center around the legitimacy of the Christian's taking an oath. This denatures the passage and misses the whole drive of it. Jesus was the Great Simplification. He was the simplification of God —reducing complicated philosophies about God, to God as Father; the simplification of life, of needs, of speech. This reduction of complicated swearing to simple straightforward speech is in line with the reduction of complicated living to simplicity, to transparency. Simplification of speech was a symbol of the inner simplification of life. Evil is complication—lies cover lies, underhand intrigues follow underhand intrigues; but the good is simple, straightforward, open, frank, and utterly truthful—"whatsoever is more than these is of the evil one."

One of the members of the Secret Police told me that one of the greatest things that Gandhi had done was to bring the nationalist movement, which had been underground in the cult of the bomb and revolutionary intrigue, out into the open. The policeman added, "Now we simply go to their headquarters and ask them what is their next move and they tell us just what they will do next and it always turns out that they have told us the truth." This is certainly sheer national gain.

Jesus came into a world of complicated swearing. If men swore by the Temple, it was nothing; but if they swore by the gold of the Temple, it was binding; if they swore by the altar, it was nothing; but if they swore by the gift on the altar, it had to be fulfilled. Jesus brushed all this casuistry aside and said: "Swear not at all. . . . Let your speech be Yea, yea, Nay, nay." Repeat for emphasis if necessary, but anything else is departing from the inner simplicity he was trying to impart to a tangled world. He knew that oaths were of no use —a good man would not need one, and a bad man would not heed one. He brushed them aside, for he knew that nothing extraneous will produce truth if a man is not inwardly truthful.

Islam is shot through and through with this complicated swearing. In the midst of my writing this chapter a Moslem came to talk with me, and to impress upon me that he had found all that I had and more, he said, "I'll swear that I have had fellowship with Christ." I quietly asked him if he had learned to swear from fellowship with the Christ, who had said, "Swear not at all."

This reverence for truth, which is so characteristic of Jesus, is at home in the atmosphere of modern science where there is a passion for truth. The most beautiful thing about modern science is not its discoveries, great as they are, but its attitude of mind, its love of truth, of frankness, its preciseness of vocabulary, its humility and its willingness to follow the facts to whatever end they may lead. There are exceptions, of course, but in general this has been the spirit of science. I think Jesus would say to the modern scientist who has this spirit of humility and love of truth, "Thou art not far from the kingdom of God." It is no mere chance that the Johns Hopkins University, a university known for its thoroughness and its scientific passion, should put over its portals the words of Jesus, "Ye shall know the truth, and the truth shall make you free"—a saying that exactly expresses the true scientific attitude.

Christ produces the very type of mind that turns on him and his gospel in reverent criticism. He is bearing the brunt of the anti-religious movement throughout the world. It is falling on him, for he produces the very kind of mind that inquires. And he can stand it! It is no mere chance that with the rediscovery of Christ during the last century there has been a rediscovery of the scientific method, nor that only where Christ is known has the scientific spirit been developed. Nor is it a mere chance that during the greatest growth of the scientific spirit there has been a growing ascendency of Christ over the minds of men— over the minds of men who possess the scientific spirit. Science now swings back to faith because faith has Christ as its center, and the very essence of that Christ is love of truth and reality. It did not just happen that the one-price system is known only where Christ is known, and that it was introduced by the Quakers, who perhaps more than any other group have embodied the mind of Christ and have embodied this demand of Christ for utter truth in speech. It is infinite gain that religion has at its center One who is crystal clear, one into whose soul we can look and find nothing there save utter honesty and truth.

I wish I could say this of all religion, but I cannot. When I ask students if it is ever right to lie, I get such answers: "Yes, in politics," "In business," "To save a life," "To support a noble cause," "In war." I do not blame them, for the gods themselves are filled with lies and intrigues, hence there are no standards. One sacred book says it is right to lie under seven conditions and another under four. A Hindu magistrate could say to me: "You cannot blame students too much for cheating, for what standards of right and wrong have we? It is all a matter of what is legal and what is not. Morals are only relative." A Moslem leader, one of the most prominent in the world, said to me with a laugh: "Oh, yes, we have a code of lies in politics. We do not take each others' statements at their face value. We know the code."

Let us look at the five conditions under which the students said that lies were justifiable. First, that it is right to lie in politics. I could answer by saying that a country progresses by the mutual confidence we have in each other's character; that a lie breaks that confidence and that a lie is, therefore, the most dangerous enemy to the national life; that no liar could be a patriot and no patriot could be a liar. As to the second, that it is right to lie in business, I could answer, that business founded on lies will sooner or later break itself upon the moral facts of the universe, for the universe is not built for the success of a lie, hence no lie or liar can finally succeed. In answer to the third, I could say that it would be far better to give one's own life, for when one lies, character is gone, and when character is gone, life is already dead. With regard to the fourth I could say that no noble cause can be served except by noble character—"Shall I do evil that good may come? God forbid." And, finally, in regard to the fifth I could say that the moral foundations of war themselves are rotten and wrong, and thus it is unfair to build up a false moral condition and say that it is right to lie in that false moral condition. I could say explicitly that a lie is never justifiable and that truth is always inviolable, and I could say it on the authority of the mind and spirit of the Master. As Speer suggests: Hold two principles within the mind and heart: First, God cannot lie, and second, he cannot delegate to you the privilege of lying for him.

When one thinks, as some do, that the ability to lie is an asset in the life, the answer is that the ability to lie is a liability and not an asset. For the universe is against it. Lies and weakness are one, truth and power are one. "Then," said a Hindu student to me after I had repeated this sentence to him, "if that is true, I do not have to think about the power aspects of my life, I have only to think about the truth aspects and the power aspects will take care of themselves." He was right and had learned a simple, but eternally great secret.

I once listened to a noted Christian controversialist carrying on a debate with an Arya

Samajist. He asked the Arya a question in long, Arabic phrases which the Arya was endeavoring to answer. When he was through, the Christian arose in his large proportioned dignity and floored his opponent with this statement: "If you can prove that you even understood my question, let alone answering it, I will become an Arya." The crowd applauded, but I think Jesus would have wept over this travesty of religion, for they were each trying to gain victory by mental gymnastics and complicated speech instead of trying to find truth by open simplicity.

An ex-headhunter of whom I heard in Assam had discovered far more of the mind of Christ than the learned apologist had ever dreamed of knowing. Among the Khassias of the Assam hills, the kingship, or seimship as it is called, of this now progressive people, who live in a very fruitful land, was to be given to a man who was in the line of succession. He was a Christian, but the darbar, made up of non-Christians and Christians, all asked for him. The position carried a great deal of honor and wealth, but he told them that he could not accept it, for it would mean that he would have to go through with the ceremonies and sacrifices involved in becoming king, and they were pagan. He was a Christian. They met again and told him that inwardly he could be opposed to these ceremonies, but let him go through with them as a mere matter of form. He replied that he could not, for it would be mental and spiritual dishonesty. He turned down a kingship because his Master had taught him to be inwardly honest. During the balance of his days he lived on about fifteen rupees, or five dollars, a month as an ordinary Christian. An ordinary Christian? Tall son of God, your spirit is regal in refusing regal honors and dignity, and if in the next life I can get near enough to you, I should like to sit at your feet and learn from you more of the mind of the Master.

Jesus exemplified and taught that simple straightforwardness that loathes complications of speech, of manner, of life. The Jews had 672 laws of moral conduct, Jesus reduced them to two—love to God and love to man. He found Martha "anxious and troubled about many things," and said to her according to the marginal reading, "But few things are needful, or one." This call to simplicity of life has been placed in the margin, not only in the margin of the Bible, but in the margin of our lives. Complexities hold the center. The call of Jesus is to bring in this love of simplicity from the margin to the center, so that we may be saved from an age that is cluttered up with things and often choked to death by them. Riches may be in the abundance of one's possessions, or may be in the fewness of one's wants. There are those who, having wells of life within, are not dependent on things. They are rich within.

Jesus said to Nathanael that he was "an Israel-ite indeed, in whom there" was "no guile," and then added, "Ye shall see the heaven opened." Yes, the secrets of heaven are open to those who are simple of heart and straightforward, and, we may add, the secrets of the earth also. Everything in heaven and earth is open to the man who himself is open. It is only as we become as little children—frank, open, simple, that the kingdom of heaven or the kingdom of the earth is open to us. Jesus is the great simplification, and he would simplify us to make us great.

.   .   .   .

To this chapter we must add a brief note on the reverence for the personality of those in economic need. It is out of the proper order, but it can probably be dealt with better at this place than in its regular order, for there it comes between two kindred thoughts of turning the other cheek and of loving one's enemies. "Give to him that asketh thee, and from him that would borrow of thee, turn not thou away" (verse 42). "An impossible command," you say. "If we gave to him that asked, and turned not away from him that would borrow, how could the economic life of the world go on? This would reduce the Christian into being as rare as the white crow of Mesopotamia. We cannot take Jesus literally." Yes, but we can! The difficulty is that we have not taken him literally, but have made him say something that he did not say, namely,

"Give to him that asketh thee everything that he asks." Jesus did not say that, for this would be ruinous both to him and to you. What he did say was: "Give to him that asketh"—not necessarily what he asks, but be so full that you will give him something, perhaps more than he asks —and better. His real need may be money—then give to him, not necessarily *all* that he asks, for that might conflict with the legitimate askings of one's own family, but give to him. He may ask you for money, and you may see that merely to give him money is a cheap and easy and ruinous way out. You must give him more—you must give him the disposition, if possible, to stand on his own feet and be self-respecting. Jesus himself did not give the man his request when he asked him to divide his brother's inheritance, but he did give to him—he gave him something that he needed more than the inheritance, namely, sound teaching about covetousness.

Every man's case, in the thought of Jesus, is your concern. Don't turn away from any man saying that you have nothing to give or to lend —you have. If you are Christ's you have something to contribute to that man's need. Jesus reiterates here what he insisted upon in the parable of the good Samaritan: you must not pass by on the other side from human need. Every man's need is your concern.

Beggars and borrowers are the economic prodigals of society. You do not turn moral and spiritual prodigals away empty. Then "give to him that asketh"—not necessarily what he asks, but what he needs, perhaps the infusion of a new spirit that will save him from his prodigality. You redeem others, then redeem him. Give to everybody, and don't give up anybody!

CHAPTER XI

REVERENCE FOR THE PERSONALITIES OF OUR ENEMIES

WHEN I come to the following verses I breathe a little faster, for we now have reached the very crux of the whole Sermon on the Mount. This refusal to retaliate, the turning of the other cheek, and the loving of one's enemies are the center of the whole. If this principle is not workable, then the heart of the sermon does not beat—it is a carcass, a dead body of doctrine. If it is workable and every other way that cuts across it is unworkable, then its heart does beat, and beating it pumps its warm lifeblood into every portion of the Christian soul and of Christian society and makes them live.

"Ye have heard that it was said, An eye for an eye, and a tooth for a tooth: but I say unto you, Resist not him that is evil: but whosoever smiteth thee on thy right cheek, turn to him the other also. And if any man would go to law with thee, and take away thy coat, let him have thy cloak also. And whosoever shall compel thee to go one mile, go with him twain. . . . Ye have heard that it was said, Thou shalt love thy neighbor and hate thine enemy: but I say unto you, Love your enemies, and pray for them

that persecute you: that ye may be sons of your
Father, . . . for he maketh his sun to rise on
the evil and the good, and sendeth rain on the
just and the unjust. For if ye love them that
love you, what reward have ye? do not even the
publicans the same? And if ye salute your
brethren only, what do ye more than others? Do
not even the Gentiles the same?" (verses 38-
48).

Here Jesus enlarges his insistence upon reverence for personality to include the personalities of those who are socially above us and can
flick our cheeks, and of those who are in power
above us and can compel us to go the forced
labor of one mile, and of those who are our
enemies. I say "flick our cheek," for it is obvious
that if a man strikes you on the right cheek with
his right hand, it must be a back-hand slap, so
that the blow does not merely represent a physical hurt, but being a blow of contempt it represents a hurt to mind and soul, to one's self-
respect. To turn the other cheek in that case is
asking a good deal of human nature. But Jesus
being what he was and wanting to do for and
with his followers what he had laid out to do,
could not ask less of them. He would lead them
to the supreme victory.

The Jewish law of "an eye for an eye and a
tooth for a tooth" limited revenge to the exact
equivalent—one eye for one eye and one tooth for
one tooth. Before that it was unlimited, so that

if a man knocked out one tooth of yours, then you were to knock out as many as you could of his. The Jewish law limited revenge; Jesus abolished it.

The doctrine of an eye for an eye and a tooth for a tooth is the Jewish expression of the law of karma. This law expresses an exact legal justice and presupposes that the universe is grounded in legal justice. The teaching that we are actively to forgive injuries presupposes that the universe goes beyond legal justice and is grounded in love. It presupposes that man is to be governed, not by legal attitudes, but by love attitudes. In doing so he strikes the deepest notes in the universe. There are three stages of human progress in reference to this matter: 1. Unlimited revenge—the law of the jungle. 2. Limited revenge—the law of karma. 3. Unlimited good will—the law of love. Portions of mankind still live under the law of karma. In fact, our legal codes are enacted upon this law —so much deed, so much penalty. This legal law takes no cognizance of the doer, only of the deed. The legal system would restrain the deed; Jesus would constrain the doer. Law touches the surface, love touches the center; one is retributive, the other is redemptive.

Jesus applies this law of love to three cases, which are, as Findlay points out: "one in which the matter at issue is not serious enough to be taken into the courts; the second in which it has been taken into the courts and there has been a serious miscarriage of justice; the last in which the normal processes of justice have been suspended by what is called by a contradiction of terms, martial law." I think the last needs correcting, for this indignity was probably not under law that was martial, but under law that was partial, where a government lays hold of certain classes, as is often done in the East and makes them do forced labor. In each case, there is deep wrong. What should be done? The temptation is to use the weapons of the wrongdoer, to fight on his level and to give blow for blow. Don't do it, said Jesus, for if you do, then blows will beget blows, hate will beget hate, and you will find yourself in a vicious circle. Get out of it by rising to a higher level and by using higher weapons—the level of unfailing love and the weapons of unquenchable good will.

Jesus is not teaching passive resistance, but an active resistance on a higher level. The account does not say, "If a man smite you on one cheek, let him smite the other also," but it does say, "Turn to him the other also." It is this audacious offensive of love that forces the man to go further and thus to break down. He tries to break your head, and you, as a Christian, try to break his heart. In turning the other cheek you wrest the offensive from him and assume moral charge of the situation. You choose your own battleground, and your own weapons, you

refuse his and compel him to stand on ground
with which he is not familiar and to face weapons
he does not know how to face. If a man compels you to go with him one mile, you are his
slave; but if you voluntarily go with him two,
then you rise from your slavery, confer a bounty
on him and thus become his master. If he sues
you at law and takes away your coat, you are
his servant, but if you confer on him your cloak
also, you assume the mastery by your own moral
daring.

Allowing a man to smite you on one cheek,
and letting him have the coat, and submitting
to him when he compels you to go one mile does
little or no good. The fact is that it does harm
to the man who does it and to the man who submits to it. It is the other cheek, the cloak also
and the second mile that do the trick. It is this
plus that turns the scale. The one cheek, the coat
and the one mile—this is passive resistance; but
turning the other cheek, giving the cloak also and
going the second mile—this is an active resistance on the plane of unquenchable good will.
Passive resistance may reveal nothing but weakness; this active resistance of love reveals nothing but strength.

When the battle closed in between Jesus and
the Jewish and Roman authorities, he was not
passive. He was entirely active and assumed
moral command in every situation. When they
came to arrest him in the garden, and Peter with

his sword struck off the ear of the servant of the high priest, using the same weapons as his enemies, Jesus rebuked Peter and pronounced the doom of those who came to arrest him with swords by saying, "They that take the sword shall perish with the sword." They came to arrest him and get sentence against him, and the first thing they confronted was the fact that they heard the sentence of doom passed upon themselves. He then assumes further moral command by stooping down, picking up the severed ear of his enemy and restoring it. In the moment of passing under their power he arises in sublimity, assumes moral command and stands, not as a helpless prisoner, but as a giver of bounty. He is before Pilate, crowned with thorns, a stick in his hand, and a mock robe of royalty about his shoulders—an object of abject pity. But is he? There shines through this abjectness a regal dignity. Pilate knew that the Prisoner was judging the judge, and "he was the more afraid." Herod had seen men gain the ascendency in his court by words, but he saw something utterly new when Jesus gained the moral command of the situation in the court by silence—a silence that hurt. When Jesus hung on the cross, he was in moral command. Instead of asking for mercy at the hands of the mob, he commends them to mercy at the hands of the Father. They put royal soldiers on guard at the tomb, and a royal seal on the tomb, but what can royal soldiers and royal seals do before a regal spirit? The final result of the issue between the two was this: "The soldiers were as dead men," but he could say, "I am the resurrection and the life." Is this power? It is the only power!

"Why didn't Jesus strike back when he was struck on the cheek at the judgment hall? Didn't he have a just right to do so?" asked a Hindu at question time.

"Yes," I replied, "I suppose he did have a just right to strike back; but if he had done so, I would not be talking about him to-night. He would be too much like me. But he turned the other cheek, and where did the blow fall—on the other cheek? No, no—on your heart and mine."

That is power—supreme power, the only real power. Had he struck one blow in return, it would have been the death-blow to his own gospel. For Christ conquers not by the quantity of his muscle, but by the quality of his spirit. Had he struck back, the blow with which he struck others would have struck him and at the same moment would have smitten to the earth every hope that we had placed in him. But, thank God, he refused their weapons and used his own. And we are at his feet.

Jesus, therefore, calls men to a new warfare, on a new plane with new weapons. It is the moral equivalent of war. He calls men to the overcoming of evil, of hate, of the world, in the only possible way that it can be done, namely, the overcoming of evil with good, of hate by love and the world by a cross. Ellwood says that "experience has shown that the only way to correct a wrong idea is by presenting a right idea." Can Satan cast out Satan? Can I by acting like the devil get the devil out of people? War is an attempt to act like the devil in order to get the devil out of people. It cannot be done. The devil sits all the tighter, for he knows these weapons—they are his very own. "A war to end war" is the supreme moral absurdity. War always has produced war and always will, by the very law that like produces like.

Don't take your code of action from the attitudes of the other man, said Jesus, in asking us to turn the other cheek. Don't let his actions determine how you shall act. Always be animated by invincible good will, no matter what he does. Be determined from within. You are not then the slave of the passing moods and attitudes of another. Marcus Aurelius was right when he said that "the only way to avenge yourself is not to become like the wrongdoer."

We have been afraid of the phrase, "Too proud to fight," because we have felt that under the cloak of this pride lurked a cowardice. The phrase must be amended to read, "Too proud to fight—with his weapons." The man who follows Jesus' way does fight—but on a higher level and with new weapons: on the level of good will and with the weapons of an inexhaustible love. This is not a gospel for the weak, but for the strong. Anyone can strike back—that shows little strength. Real strength is shown when a man is strong enough to strike back, but is also strong enough to refrain from striking back on that level. The soldiers of Cromwell recognized this kind of strength when they went to arrest George Fox, the Quaker, for preaching against war. He turned on them and preached to them so daringly that they involuntarily exclaimed, "You are the man for our officer, come and join us." And Pilate, used to seeing emperors in triumphal entries, exclaimed as he saw Jesus: "Behold the man!" This was real manhood, the supreme manhood!

Let us get the issue clear. The statement of Jesus does not say, "If a man strike your child on its cheek, you are to turn the child's other cheek also." In that case I would have a duty to society to protect society with my life. Where the offense is personal and against me, I am to bear it and to conquer by other weapons. But how about this duty we owe to society? Can we use force in that case? Is a police force justifiable? We would answer "Yes," under the present conditions of human society. Since society as a whole, or on a widespread scale, is not yet able to use these higher weapons of love-restraint, they must use the weapons of force-restraint. But even this does not make war justifiable, for there is a distinct difference between a police force and an army, trained for war. A police force is not trained against another police force; it is trained against criminals. A police force is for the purpose of apprehending the guilty and the guilty alone. But an army does not pretend to apprehend the guilty. It destroys the innocent and the guilty alike. Those guilty in war are seldom or never apprehended. A police force brings the criminal to the processes of law and justice; an army does not strive to bring the guilty to processes of law and justice, but to settle things by the arbitration of force. The objectives, then, are different: one looks to the arbitrament of right, the other to the arbitrament of might.

We have said above that society was not prepared for the use of these higher weapons, but we have seen an attempt to use them in the nationalist movement in India under Mahatma Gandhi. For the first time in human history, on a widespread scale, a nation in the attainment of its national ends has repudiated force and has substituted the power of suffering, or soul-force. Granting that violence did creep in here and there, the amazing thing is that, considering the numbers involved and the almost certain coming into the movement of elements that had not assimilated its inner principles, such a small amount of violence was manifested. I know of no struggle for national freedom recounted in history that was so good-tempered, that left behind it so little bitterness and hate and that was so purifying to the people who partook in it. When Easter day came the Congress "Dictator" of Behar, Rajendra Pershad, a Hindu, sent word to the British superintendent of police that, since that day was Easter, and since he would probably desire to go to church, they would call off their activities for that day to allow him to do so!

As the British superintendent of police was searching the beautiful home of Doctor Ansari, one of the very finest of Moslem congressmen, for incriminating evidence, tea time came. Doctor Ansari invited the Englishman to have tea with him. (I had tea in that very room a few weeks before; it was good tea, too, and the host was a prince.) This doctor, accustomed to the greatest luxuries, marches off to jail, his only crime being that he is a member of the Congress Committee which had been proscribed—and he does it with a smile! There is something irresistible in a movement when the people belonging to it gladly go to jail, stand up under lathi blows and conquer their conquerors by their unconquerable spirit. It has been objected that the movement caused great economic damage to India by the upsetting of normal trade, etc. But the loss from the temporary upsetting of trade is nothing to the gain of a nation shedding its fears, its inferiority complexes, and its slave-mentality.

The world owes to India a deep debt of gratitude in that it has shown a method by which the dispossessed in any realm can gain their rights without resorting to war. Perhaps in this movement the world has turned a corner.

If the world ever abolishes war, then it will owe that deliverance to three men more than to any others: To Woodrow Wilson, the creator of the League where national clashes can be resolved by Conference; to Salmon O. Levinson, the man who conceived the idea that war is not mere calamity, but is crime, and who inspired the nations to sign the pact renouncing war as collective sin; and to Gandhi, who, when the principles and practices of neither League nor Pact could be applied, showed that there is a moral process for dealing with a situation which hitherto has been relegated to war. To these three men—one a Christian, one a Jew, and one a Hindu—the world owes a debt of gratitude and love.

And yet—and yet—behind these three men stood a Man who enunciated on a hilltop two thousand years ago the principles which, on the one hand, have haunted the hearts and councils of fighting men, and on the other, have inspired the councils of men of good will to the unquenchable hope that his dream is not a dream, but the only sane reality that will get men out of the insanity of war. This Man, sometimes despised and put aside as a weakling, sometimes disguised and put in front as a warrior, but always reappearing as neither, has been the persisting, haunting Issue. He enunciated the principles in the Sermon on the Mount and exemplified their practice in the mount called Calvary. He showed there the supreme conquest—the overcoming of evil with good, of hate by love, and of the world by a cross.

"Aren't we non-Christians more Christian than you Christians in that we act on the principles and methods of Jesus and you don't?" has been asked again and again at the question hour since this movement began. I have had to answer that the method that Gandhi and his followers have adopted is very closely akin to the method of the Sermon on the Mount, and in acting on this they have been more Christian than we have usually been. And yet I cannot identify the two methods —the method of Civil Disobedience and the method of the Sermon on the Mount. When constitutional means are not open there are three ways by which righteous ends may be gained apart from war—Passive Resistance, Civil Disobedience, and the Method of Jesus. Passive Resistance is the method of bearing passively imposed wrongs and penalties in the hope of calling attention to the wrongs and thus gaining redress. Civil Disobedience is the choosing of certain laws and regulations to be disobeyed in order that by their disobedience and the bearing of consequent suffering, a larger end may be gained in the changing of the whole system of which these particular oppressive laws and regulations are thought to be representative. The difference between Passive Resistance and Civil Disobedience may be illustrated thus: It is Passive Resistance when a man drafted for war refuses to be drafted and goes to jail instead; it is Civil Disobedience when a man, opposed to war in general and desiring to oppose it, chooses the draft law as the test-point, deliberately breaks it before it actually touches him and tries to get others to do the same. The one is passive and personal, the other is active and collective. The one chooses to break the law when it is specifically imposed, the other chooses the law to be broken when not specifically imposed on him.

The method of Jesus is different from either and yet it sums up both and goes beyond each. It has within it the passive elements of the first and the active elements of the second, but it adds a third—an active offensive of love on a higher level. Passively bearing a wrong is not enough; nor is going out and precipitating a crisis in order to bear the penalty of that precipitation enough. You must add an element, the vital element that may be lacking in each—the active and audacious offensive of love. Without this element the whole thing will fail. It is this plus that puts soul into it.

Because this element of active love has been absent very often in the Civil Disobedience movement many an Englishman fighting on the other side could see nothing but lawlessness in the act of civil disobedience. He met the breaking of law by the imposing of the penalty of law and felt that he was righteous in doing so. And especially did he feel that way when in the faces and attitudes of the civil resisters he could see only hate toward him. He was untouched, for the thing that might have touched him was not there, namely, an active love.

It is for this reason that Jesus, after talking about turning the other cheek and going the second mile, immediately adds that we are to love our enemies and do good to them that despitefully use us. He links the passive resistance of evil and the active love of the enemy who does the evil and makes them one. Without this active love the method of conquering by turning the other cheek is savorless salt. It may do harm. Without this active love, going one mile, and even going two, may do harm to the oppressor and the oppressed in that it may produce contempt in the mind of the oppressor and may further weaken the oppressed. One may allow himself to be smitten on the other cheek, but in his heart of hearts he may be saying, "Yes, but I hate you and will get even with you if I can." That kills the active element that would work on the heart of the oppressor and renders the method sterile. Love gives the method life. That which made the death of Jesus different, in addition to the character of the sufferer, was the fact that out from him went an active love toward the men that put him to death and which expressed itself in the prayer for his enemies, "Father, forgive them." That spirit wrested the offensive from their hands and turned the tragedy into a triumph.

The movement of Gandhi has succeeded—gloriously succeeded, in so far as it has embodied this active element of good will, which it has actually done in the case of Gandhi himself and many of his followers who have caught his spirit. It has failed in so far as it has taken the method of Gandhi without the element of good will toward the British. A member of the Calcutta Congress said to a friend of mine, "It was a glorious Congress—there was a lot of hate." It was this spirit that broke it down again and again. Where the movement existed on hate it failed in everything except to stiffen the opponent the more; where it existed on good will there it won sympathy, then an honest examination of the alleged wrongs, and then final success.

Two sets of people look on this movement: one looks at the underlying hate and the outward breaking of the law and pronounces the movement wrong and a failure; the other set looks at the glorious spirit of unabated good will in the actions of Gandhi and his followers and pronounce it the most glorious national success ever attained. In a way both are right. As the movement has been mixed, so the effect has been mixed. But on the whole I find it the most purifying, the most heroic and the most successful movement ever inaugurated on such a scale—and the most nearly Christian.

There are those who question whether one as a Christian ever has a right to break with constituted authority. For did not Jesus say, "Render to Cæsar that which is Cæsar's"? Many a vested wrong has nestled up under this verse for protection and sanction on the implication that Jesus meant that whatever is in government is right and must be supported as such. This would mean that the Christian must always stand behind the *status quo*—obviously an impossible position. The Christian of all men is out for a new world, this would make him only a court chaplain to the old. Jesus did say, "Render to Cæsar that which is Cæsar's," but he went on and added, "Render to God that which is God's." In doing so he laid down alongside of rendering to Cæsar that which is Cæsar's the oft-times incompatible principle of rendering to God that which is God's. In his teaching concerning the kingdom of God he unfolded the fact that we were to render all life to God—personal, economic, social and political—for God was to be King of all. As he thus enlarged the border of what belonged to God, soon there was no standing room for Cæsar. He was pushed out, for he could not fit into the ideal of rendering to God that which is God's. If rendering to Cæsar is compatible with rendering to God, then Cæsar may stay; if not, then Cæsar must go. This coin has Cæsar's image stamped upon it. You have God's image stamped upon you. Then give to Cæsar money, but give yourself to God. But if giving money to Cæsar cuts across the giving yourself to God, then, of course, God has the highest allegiance and Cæsar must go. "Every plant that my heavenly Father hath not planted shall be rooted up," including Cæsar, if Cæsar is a weed in the soil of the garden of the kingdom of God. In that second part of the statement Jesus laid down a most revolutionary principle —a principle that has already been responsible for a lot of Cæsars being ousted, with many more to follow, until the kingdoms of this world shall become compatible with and synonymous with the kingdom of our God and his Christ.

It is often the painful duty of the Christian to break with Cæsar in order to keep step with God. Often he must break with laws in order to be true to Law. By "Law" we mean that abstract rule of right lying behind and above laws. All laws do not conform to Law; very often they contradict. To the degree that laws conform to Law we are under obligation to obey them. When to the Christian there is a conflict between laws and Law, he must break with society at the level of the unrighteous laws in order to meet

society at the level of Law. The end is not a
permanent break, but only a break in order to a
higher union. By the break and the consequent
suffering the Christian hopes to lift society to the
higher level. The fact is that this is often the
only method by which society can be lifted. For
wherever society has taken a higher road you will
find at the junction of the lower and the higher
road somebody's cross of pain.

Jesus insists that we take the same method
of dealing with our relationships in the limited
circle as he took in the larger, infinite relationships, namely, the method of the cross. There are
those who feel that the Sermon on the Mount is
not a complete way of life, since the cross is not
in it. It is quite true that not everything in
Christianity is found in the Sermon, but certainly the cross is not absent. What are conquering by turning the other cheek and going
the second mile and overcoming by your own
suffering but the method of the cross? Here
in the Sermon on the Mount is our cross, while at
Mount Calvary is his cross, and we are willing
to trust the one and unwilling to try the other.
The tragedy of Christianity through the centuries is that it has taken the cross of Christ
for its creed but anything else but the Sermon
on the Mount for its deed. We are not as honest as the British minister in charge of the navy,
who, when his navy was being curtailed and reduced, objected in these words: "You make me

give up this navy which I have fostered and watched grow as a father would his own child, you make me give it up in loyalty to Christ whom I do not love, and make me disloyal to Jehovah, God of battles, whom I do love."

"Try this method of love on the tiger and see what will happen," said a questioner one day in order to floor me. He was quite right. It would not work on a tiger. But it will work on a man. This believing that a man will respond to the force of an offensive on the plane of love is a most amazing adventure in faith in human nature. The underlying assumption is that in every man there are two men—one that is evil, whom you are not to resist, on his level, with his weapons—"resist not him that is evil"—and another man, who is not evil, but who is susceptible to the appeal of loving suffering. Get to that man and you win, said Jesus. No, it will not work with a tiger, but Jesus' assumption is that men are not tigers, and there is that in every man which is capable of response. Even if he does not respond and the method fails, still you have grown tall in the process of stooping. You win in either case.

Retaliation always loses, even when it seems to win. In a church quarrel in South India over the right to a large amount of property, those on one side, to gain their point, called in the Bishop of Antioch and said that their churches were vested in him. They won. They never dreamed that the Bishop of Antioch would be other than a figure-head with which they could win their case. Instead, however, he now steps in and claims control of his property! They are spending hundreds of thousands of rupees in more court cases to get rid of him! If you take the method of retaliation, you call in a spirit that takes control of the situation and you will pass under its dominance. You will be like the sorcerer's apprentice who came in distress to his master and said, "Sir, I have called up a spirit and now I cannot rid myself of him." The only possible way to get rid of the spirit of retaliation is by the spirit of forgiveness and good will. The essential Christian spirit is the spirit of refusal to retaliate, an active and inexhaustible forgiveness of injuries. It was the beautiful thing in the cross, it is the most beautiful thing in the Christian. If we fail here, we fail as Christians.

"Why do Christian nations go to war and fight?" a Hindu asked me one day.

"For the same reason that you and other people fight," I replied.

"Yes, but they are Christians," he concluded in a tone that was final.

Another said to me: "You Christians and we Hindus should change sacred books. You should take the Gita, for it approves war, and we should take the New Testament, for it is opposed to it. This would suit us both better."

I was holding a decision meeting with students in a camp far from the noise and disturbance of the city. At a very critical moment, when I was pressing home the claims of Christ upon the awakened minds and hearts of these youths, some Europeans began banging away at ducks on a pond near by. It was very disconcerting. Western guns were disturbing the Christian appeal to the East! It is a fact that the sound of the booming of guns and the noise of the preparation for war in the West break in upon us as we make our Christian appeal to India, for India knows that this is utterly unchristian. Especially now does all this war-mentality seem incongruous to India because she herself has discovered a way that demonstrates the effectiveness of the Christian way. The non-Christians themselves are recognizing this as the essential Christian spirit. "I am afraid I did not show the Christian spirit in that matter," said a Pārsee to a friend of mine in reference to this matter of retaliation.

It may be that the East will yet teach this spirit to the West. Some Christians from among the Nagas (the dog-eaters) of Assam were compelled by the British official to do their turn carrying his loads fifteen miles, as a punishment for not fulfilling certain orders which had conflicted with their Christian convictions. They carried the burdens the extra fifteen miles without a murmur, and then turned up the next day ready to carry them that day also. When the official asked them what they were doing there they replied: "The gospel tells us that when compelled to go one mile we are to go two. You compelled us to go one march yesterday as punishment for our convictions, we are now ready to go the two." These ex-headhunters quietly taught the Westerner—and all of us, something of the spirit of the gospel.

Contrast that story with this one: The Syrians of South India have been Christians for centuries, but except for a section of them who are very evangelical and progressive, their Christianity has petrified into dead forms. They are all very anxious to see the Host as it is raised up at the time of the communion whether they partake of the communion or not. They feel that some magic benefit comes to them from the very sight of it. They all run to the church when they hear the tolling of the bell which tells them that the Host is about to be raised. One day when the bell began tolling one of these Christians was carrying on a quarrel with his neighbor. What could he do? He wanted to see the Host, but he could not stop his quarrel. So he called to his wife to come and continue the quarrel, until he could see the Host and came back. She did! He returned in due time and resumed the quarrel! The story is ridiculous, but not more so than nations professing to be Christian piling up huge armaments, training their youth in war mentality and preparing for the next war, and then solemnly going to church to worship at the feet of the Crucified. It is not only unchristian —it is blasphemy.

There is no possible way to get rid of an enemy except to turn him into your friend, and there is no possible way to get rid of hate except by love. "Name one harlot," someone has said, "who has ever been reclaimed by treating her as a harlot." And we may add, Name one enemy who was ever reclaimed by treating him as an enemy. Treat your enemy as a friend and in the end he will be your friend; or, if he is not, you will have become a far finer man in the process. In doing this, said Jesus, "you will be sons of your Father," for these are his methods. He makes his sun to rise on the evil and the good, and sends rain on the just and on the unjust and he loves his enemies. "God's punishment is pardon. His retribution is reconciliation, his revenge is forgiveness." He rules from a cross. His method of omnipotence is the omnipotence of love.

Jesus has done the impossible about God—he has put strict moral qualities and lavish love together in the same Being. Making his sun to rise on the evil and on the good would be looseness had not the portrait of the Father been so amazingly moral that it could stand these touches of lavish love.

If you love those that love you—what do you more than others? You are to have a joy that "exceeds" (verse 11), a righteousness that "exceeds" (verse 20), and a love that "exceeds" (verses 46, 47). Jesus asks, "What do ye more?" That "more" is the Christian difference. All people are religious up to a certain point; it is this plus, this overflow, that counts. It is the overflow of the Nile that saves Egypt from being desert. We belong to the people who go beyond —beyond duties to privileges, beyond the first cheek to the second cheek, beyond the first mile to the second, beyond the coat to the cloak also, beyond the stale-mate of revenge to the victory of love.

The victory of love! Love cannot be defeated, for in its very defeat it is victorious. A young, highly intelligent and beautiful-spirited Quaker goes out to China, and after living a life of self-sacrifice is murdered by the people to whom he came. Could anything be more abject in its defeat, both for him and for the Chinese? And yet when the Chinese students chose one word, that would symbolize the whole, wrought out in flowers to lay upon his grave, they chose the word, "Victory." They were right, for a life of love is deathless, even in death, and victorious even in defeat; life is judged not by its accomplishments, but by its attitudes.

.   .   .   .

The reward of this kind of living which Jesus has been setting before us in the Sermon is in the quality of being: "Ye shall be sons of your

Father," or as Luke puts it—"sons of the Most High." Being willing to be the sons of the most low, you turn out to be sons of the Most High. The reward is in the very make-up of your character. It is not in being given a harp in heaven, but in winning a heart that has learned its song; not in being allowed to walk on streets of fine gold, but in having the refined gold of character. Your greatest reward will be that you will be like your Father. And that is heaven, whatever the future may bring. Every man will reflect himself in his environment, he will draw around him in his environment qualities like his own. Any man that takes heaven with him is bound to have heaven. But the basis of that heaven and the degree of that heaven is character.

As I have already said, in these twenty-seven marks of perfection there is not one that is irrelevant, and not one that will not be utterly necessary in the make-up of the perfect character for God and man. In the Father too? Yes. For these twenty-seven marks are in the Father himself: He is surrendered in spirit—in Christ he surrenders himself to the limitations, the trials, the buffetings and the cross of an earthly life; he mourns—the cross is the symbol of that deep vicarious mourning; he is the serving meek, if Jesus is the image of his person; he hungers and thirsts after righteousness—not in himself, but in others, in his children—the God of moral indifference has faded out and a God intensely

ethical is here. But in all his holiness he is the
merciful toward imperfections in others; he is
the pure in heart—in him is no darkness at all;
the peacemaker—an active intervener in love.
He is persecuted and falsely spoken against, yet
he rejoices and is exceedingly glad. He is the
salt of the earth—the silent power that keeps it
from corruption and that puts taste and worth
and meaning into life. The light of the world—
take him out and the world turns to night. He
keeps the least commandment that he lays on
others. He is not indifferent to the painful
struggle upward. He does not destroy it, he
fulfills it. He is not angry with his children in
the sense of revenge, but only in the sense of
redemptive, moral indignation. He is quick to
agree with his adversaries, going more than half
way. He is above all impurity, even in thought.
His word is simple and Yea, yea, and Nay, nay—
not subject to whimsicalities. He resists evil
on the high level of turning the other cheek, going
the second mile, and giving the cloak also. He
gives to them that ask and from those that would
borrow he turns not away. He loves his enemies
and does good to them that despitefully use him.
He sends the rain on the just and on the unjust,
makes the sun to rise on the evil and the good.
He loves them that do not love him and salutes
those who pass him by—he is the Perfect!

This kind of a God can have my heart. For
as Jesus has been sketching for us the likeness

of the Father I see in it his own likeness. God
is Christlike; and if he is, then he is a good God
and trustable. If a radical college president is
right when he says that "the word 'atheism' has
dropped from the vocabulary of the intelligent.
The only question is what kind of a God can
we believe in," then the kind that Jesus depicts
is morally inescapable. In one of our Round
Table Conferences an intelligent Hindu said,
"When I am in need, I turn without discrimination to any god that may be at hand." I don't.
I turn to this God whom I can morally respect
to the very depths of my being. If this is the
Heart of the universe, then he can have my heart.

Mankind has a goal that we can morally respect! Not the snuffing out of Nirvana, nor
the awful silences of the Impersonal Atma, nor
the paradise of houris, nor a cheap, easy heaven,
but to be perfect as the Father is perfect! This
is good news—a veritable gospel!

DIVIDED PERSONALITY THE REASON WE DO NOT ATTAIN THE GOAL

CHAPTER XII

INWARD DIVISIONS IN SPIRITUAL RELATIONSHIPS

AFTER placing before us perfection as the Father is perfect, as the goal of human living, Jesus now goes on and in the most incisive and, we may add, the most decisive way puts his finger on the reasons why we do not reach that goal. And after being sifted down all these reasons really come to one, namely, divided personality. He diagnoses our difficulty as inward division.

The chairman of one of my meetings, a Hindu, said, "If what the speaker has said to-night isn't true, then it doesn't matter; but if it is true, then nothing else matters." If what Jesus has been saying about the goal of life is not true, then of course it does not matter; but if it is true, then certainly nothing else matters. Everything in life should bend toward this one thing. Nothing should be tolerated that cuts across this central purpose. Everything should be at the disposal of this all-gripping fact. The thought of it should fill our horizon, it should fill us.

Jesus saw that men were not moving on to that goal for the simple reason that they did not desire it with all their beings. So he puts his finger upon the nine ways in which men are inwardly divided:

1. You do your beautiful religious acts with divided motive—you give to God, but also "to be seen of men" (chapter 6, verses 1-4).

2. You pray in two directions—to be heard of God and to be overheard of men (verses 5-15).

3. You fast with divided purpose—you do it before God and yet you hope that men will give you credit for being abstemious (verses 16-18).

4. You try to lay up treasure in two directions, upon earth and in heaven (verses 19-21).

5. You see in two directions—your outlook is divided (verses 22, 23).

6. You are trying to be loyal in two directions —trying to serve God and mammon (verse 24).

7. You are anxious in two directions—toward what you shall eat and drink and be clothed with, and also toward the kingdom of God (verses 25-34).

8. You are criticizing in two directions— toward your brother with rather heavy emphasis and toward yourself rather lightly (chapter 7, verses 1-5).

9. You are giving yourself in two directions— giving yourself to God and also giving that holy thing called personality to the dogs of appetite and the swine of desire (verse 6).

These, he said, are the causes of your failure. Note that over against the nine beatitudes, which are the foundations of spiritual success, he puts nine divisions which are the foundations of spiritual failure. The first nine strike the note of victory, the second nine strike the note of dismal defeat. If you are failing to make real progress toward the perfect life, then check over these nine causes, and among them you will find the special thing that is tripping you. They cover the field of failure.

It is interesting that modern psychologists, studying the laws of our mental being, have come to the same conclusion as to the cause of human unhappiness—we are divided against ourselves, inwardly at war. They tell us that we are mentally at strain, that there is something, perhaps in the subconscious mind, warring against the rest of us and setting up inward friction, and that this is the cause of most nervous diseases. One's only hope is to get these warring things up and out into the open and related to the rest of the man, so that inward unity may be found. This is interesting. But to the Galilæan on the hillside two thousand years ago, with his deeper insight, with surer touch, with the offer of a greater goal as an inducement to get out of these divisions, and with a sufficient dynamic in his own person as the method of arising out of them —to him we go, for in his quiet calm and poise he embodies that inner unity we so deeply crave.

As I sit writing by the Arabian seaside I cannot keep my eyes off the point just in front of me where two currents meet. Each current is struggling for the right of way with the result that in that otherwise calm sea there is an area of boiling, tossing confusion. Jesus sat and watched the confusion and strain in men's hearts and said: "Your souls are the meeting place of contradictory currents. You want mutually exclusive things, and in the end you get nowhere—nowhere except into worse confusion." He would simplify life into oneness of desire and purpose, so that it might take on calm and poise and power. For as long as life is balanced between competing ends there is weakness and inward collapse and lack of outer effectiveness. So relentlessly he puts his finger on the places where we ail.

In the first of the nine beatitudes he insists that the first step toward perfection is inward renunciation of spirit in which we cleanse away the inward competitions and contradictions and become simple and sincere. He now insists in this first of the nine causes of failure that the lack of inward simplicity and sincerity is the first step down. You give your alms—a most beautiful thing, said Jesus, but you do it "to be seen of men." Eucken says with penetrating insight that the greatest danger to religion is that the old self-life after being put out by repentance and renunciation comes back again and takes over the new forms in the service of the old self. It is the old self; the only difference is that it is now religious.

A planter's servant brought him an egg in an egg-cup. Breaking the top, he found that the egg wasn't exactly fresh, and he ordered the servant to take it away and bring another. The servant did so and the planter ate the egg, only to find when he got to the bottom that it was the same old egg, turned upside down! The application is plain. Often the old evil-smelling self comes back, clothed now in the proprieties of religion. But it is the same old self.

Jesus shows us how this self-life manifests itself in three relationships: Toward others (alms, righteousness), toward God (prayer), and toward oneself (fasting). These three religious functions practically cover the field of religion: 1. Receiving—prayer. 2. Giving—alms. 3. Self-restraints—fasting. Jesus, therefore, picked out the three outstanding things in religion, and showed how they are spoiled by a self-interest running through them. Alms, or other religious duty, plus sincerity equals a good deed, but alms, plus an eye to reward from men, equals death.

I saw a sadhu standing all day immovable, unattracted by the things going on around him. But he always chose a very prominent corner on which to stand! I visited a sadhu who sat on a bed of spikes and he was contemptuous in his indifference to me and to everyone else, but his bed of spikes was at the crossroads where the multitudes surged—and saw! One would think that a man who had no possessions, and no clothes but ashes, would care little for appearances, yet when I was about to take a picture of such a man, he objected, saying that his ashes were not on properly!

We smile at this, but this penetrating verse about not doing religious things "to be seen of men" renders a great deal of our present-day Christianity unchristian. Preaching to save souls, but also to satisfy the love of prominence; building huge churches in which to worship God, but also through this splendor trying to outshine the other denominations; giving for religious purposes, but seeing to it that the gift is prominently noted and human credit given—these things spoil the Christian character of the deed, and leave it religious, but not Christian. The Christian soul of it has died. It is a dead deed. Preaching is at once the most life-giving and the most deadly thing in the world. Waiting for compliments at the close and secretly rejoicing in them de-Christianizes the whole performance —and leaves it a performance. I once saw a notice in a paper, blocked around with such thick black lines to call attention to it, that I thought it was an obituary notice. You can call attention to yourself in religion with such emphasis that you succeed in announcing only your own spiritual death.

"You Christians are better Pharisees than you are Christians, and the ministers are not as Christian as the laity," an earnest-minded Hindu said to me. It made me wince, and it also made me think, for it is a fact that by the slightest turn we may produce Pharisees instead of Christians. The Pharisees believed that if only two people went to heaven, one would be a Pharisee and the other would be a scribe. Now the last people on earth who seemed to be in danger of Pharisaism were the group of simple, peasant fishermen who were followers of Jesus, and yet he said to them, "Beware of the leaven of the Pharisees." With deep insight and foresight he saw that the one thing that would plague his gospel would be the spirit that could repeat these wonderful things and take it for granted that because they could be repeated, they were necessarily operative in them. I once saw in a child, at collection time, the difference between the Christian and the Pharisee. In its simplicity and sweetness the child held up its copper coin and dropped it into the bag; almost all of the rest of the congregation also put in copper coins, but they put them in, not openly as the child did, but concealed within their palms and dropped deep into the bag so that perchance someone would think they had put in a silver rupee! How is it that in a Christian congregation the amount of collections will immediately go up if open plates are exchanged for bags? To be seen of men! The dominance of the herd!

In a town in New England one denomination felt that the other denomination had a bell larger and more authoritative than theirs, so they got a new one. Not to be outdone, the other also got a new one. The first-named installed a still larger bell, and the other followed suit. Then the first one put in such a big bell that, when they rang it, it cracked! All this proclaiming of one's greatness, even through religion, ends in cracked bells. The Interchurch Movement depended so much on bigness and clamor that the bell soon cracked. The trumpet of the Pharisee, both ancient and modern, which is used to call attention to religious deeds and religious greatness, simply ends in proclaiming the trumpeter's own spiritual doom.

The wife of a priest of a temple told a friend of mine that when the people came to offer their gifts before the idol in exchange for certain boons, the priest would sit behind the idol unseen and would bargain with the worshipers, who, of course thought they were hearing the voice of the god. There are some very human voices, and very human motives behind much of religion, out of which God is supposed to be speaking.

Jesus said that if a subtle desire to be seen of men runs through your doing of religious things, then the deed dies with the moment, there is no lasting quality. You wanted the praise of men —you got it. That settles the account, there is no reward with your Heavenly Father.

This brings us face to face with an objection often brought against the gospel, namely, that it is founded on reward-morality. One critic puts it this way: "The bottom has dropped out of reward-morality, so Christianity and Christian missions founded on reward-morality cease to grip the mind of this age that demands a higher basis for morality." The Hindu contrasts this so-called reward-morality of the Gospels with the Hindu doctrine of "nishkama karma"—work without desire for fruit or reward, to the discredit of the Gospels. Certainly, if the gospel is founded on a reward-morality, then its motivation is of a low type. We must acknowledge that a great many Christians, holding as they do to the idea of an imposed heaven and an imposed hell, do take it for granted that our gospel is founded on reward-morality. But run through the Sermon and the rest of the teachings of Jesus and you will find a different note. Observe that this passage, where it speaks of reward, says that you have your reward *"with* your heavenly Father." It is not "from"—that would be a handed-out, external reward, but "with"; that is, it is worked out with him, in fellowship with him and his purposes. The word "with" denotes the difference between the external and the intrinsic reward. There is bound to be result, hence reward from human action; the question is what is the nature of the reward? In the gospel it is intrinsic and not external. Note this passage in Luke's Gospel which has been translated thus: "But love your enemies and do them good, and lend, never despairing: and ye shall have a rich reward: ye shall be sons of the Most High." The reward was in the quality of the being—"ye shall *be.*" Now to "be sons of the Most High" is a quality of being—not an imposition but a disposition.

Moreover, by the very nature of the motive behind all Christian doing a reward-morality, in the lower sense, is ruled out. As Seeley has pointed out: "With a view to his ultimate interest a man may fast, may impose painful penances on himself, . . . may even go two miles instead of one, . . . may turn the other cheek, . . . may even pray for those who use him despitefully. . . . But can a man with a view to his ultimate interest love his enemies?" By the very nature of the case it is impossible. The gospel is a love-morality and hence cannot be reward-morality.

The Bhagawad Gita founded its morality on "nishkama karma," or disinterestedness, or without desire or thought for reward. It keeps insisting that there should be no thought of reward. This, however, is bad psychology, for by that very insistence that one should work without thought of reward you call attention to reward and fix it in the mind. In the doctrine of love, by the very nature of things, desire for reward cannot be a part of it, consequently there is no such insistence that there shall be no desire for reward. Love is "nishkama karma" without calling attention to it. It is therefore the right psychology. One tries to get rid of the desire for reward by constantly insisting that there shall be no such desire, the other gets rid of it by the very nature of the motive, namely, love. The one is extraneous and bad psychology, the other is intrinsic and good psychology. The one is cold and indifferent, the other is warm and winsome. One has resulted in indifferentism, the other in world-service. In the Gita the "nishkama karma" has resulted in being indifferent to the effects of one's deeds, even though those deeds be the making of others suffer even unto death on the battlefield. In the gospel love ends in suffering for others on a cross.

It is no mere chance that alongside the doctrine of "nishkama karma" there exists in the doctrine of karma the greatest system of reward-morality that the world has ever seen. Karma is reward-morality pure and simple. At a time when bubonic plague was raging a friend of mine suggested that something be done to relieve conditions. The head-man of a village, a Buddhist, replied: "Nothing can be done. It is the result of their previous karma. So do not disturb it." Some money-lenders said to that same friend when he protested against the exorbitant rates charged to the villages: "We can do nothing. These people who are suffering from these high rates are suffering from their karma. They must deserve it or it would not have come upon them."

Karma is reward-morality of the grossest kind.

In the passage in the Sermon on the Mount the word "openly" had been added by some transcriber to the sentence: "The Father shall recompense thee." The Revised Version omits it. This word had been added because the transcriber's mind was still bound up with external rewards, but the implication that comes from the rest of Jesus' words is that, since the deed is to be secret, the reward too shall be secret and intrinsic and spiritual.

There seems to be a contradiction between the verse, "Let not your left hand know what your right hand doeth," and the verse, "Let your light so shine before men that they seeing your good works may glorify the Father which is in heaven." The contradiction is only seeming, for Jesus is not speaking against doing good deeds before men, but the doing of good deeds "to be seen of men" for them to glorify us. If the purpose of letting the light shine is that the people glorify the Father and not us, then the deed has a Christian motive behind it.

*   *   *   *   *   *   *   *

In this chapter Jesus mentions two other relationships in which we are divided in motive—in prayer, which has relationship with God, and in fasting, which has relationship with ourselves. Prayer is the most delicately beautiful exercise of the Christian. To him at one moment prayer is aspiration on its knees, in the next moment it is "effort on its knees." The rhythm of inflow and overflow is the heartbeat of the Christian. Never did words frame more beautiful aspiration than when Jesus taught our trembling lips to say, "Our Father." In just two words he taught us the brotherhood of man—"Our," and the Fatherhood of God—"Father." By one simple stroke, "May thy kingdom come and may thy will be done on earth as it is done in heaven," he brought religion down from

> "Screwing itself up so high,
>   For anything beneath the sky,"

and made it the most challenging, the most radical, and the most living issue ever presented to the minds of men. The kingdom of God on earth! A new personal, social, economic, political, and cosmic order knocking, ever knocking at the door of Things-as-they-are. It is the Ought-to-be standing and confronting the Is. Were ever such disturbing, savingly disturbing, words ever put within the lips of aspiring man? And when he ends the whole statement on prayer with the words that, if we expect the Heavenly Father to forgive us, then we must forgive our brother also, he put together the tenderest humanism and the truest religion and made them one.

Yet all of this can be spoiled, utterly spoiled, by using this sacred exercise for a sordid purpose—the purpose of the old self-life. That old self-life can crawl serpent-like across our most

sacred moments. We can make prayer a parade.
There is a picture in one of the Galleries, which
seems at first sight to be a monk standing in reverent devotion with folded hands, but when you
get nearer you see that he is squeezing a lemon
into a punch bowl. Much of religion seems rever-
ential at a distance, but when we get closer, we
find that it is used in the purpose of the self. "The
Pharisee stood and prayed with himself," yes,
with himself and for himself in the purposes of
the self. I was once invited to be one of three
who should offer a prayer for the success of the
Allied arms. The other two were a Hindu pundit
and a Moslem maulvi. At that time, I am
ashamed to say, I was caught by the war mentality and had not arrived even as far as the Welsh
deacon who was heard to pray: "O God, we are
at war. Help us in this fight. We know the
Germans are also praying to thee for thee to help
them. What canst thou do? O Lord, at least remain neutral." I was not interested in God's
remaining neutral—I wanted him to help us!
But the point I wish to make is connected with
the programs, on which was printed: "Speeches
by way of Prayers: Maulvi so and so, Pandit so
and so, and Rev. E. Stanley Jones." Speeches
by way of prayers—I've been guilty of just that,
I suppose, full many a time, and yet it did shock
me to see it in print!

Present-day Christianity, gazing into the mir-
ror that Jesus sets up of the man standing at the

street corner to be seen of men, is not proud of what it sees—the image of its own externalism and of its own self-seeking. And it knows in its heart of hearts that the image is not Christian.

.   .   .   .

Jesus now emphasizes a third relationship in which we spoil our finest deeds and attitudes by cross-currents of interests, namely, the relationship to ourselves. We fast to be seen of men— we refrain for a self-interest. Real religion enables a man to restrain and to refrain. Through it a man learns to say "No" to the immediate, in order to say "Yes" to the imperishable. So the Christian picks out an imperious appetite like hunger and restrains its demands in order to show that he is master and not servant. This is deeply needed in modern life, for most of us are the bellhops of our appetites. The consequence is that "God is fattened out of us." Real religion enables a man to restrain his desires and not resign to them. But, says Jesus, you may spoil this beautiful act of physical restraint by using that very restraint for the purposes of spiritual show. You start out to suppress the physical, and end in expressing the old self-life. In one place in India the rich men of the city start out each year with bands and banners to walk to a distant shrine on foot—a very arduous journey. The bands and banners announce the renunciation and the piety. But after going a few miles beyond the city these rich men invariably turn back and take the train and ride to the sacred place in comfort. Many of us start out with a great show of self-renunciation and end in self-pampering. We renounce everything to come into the ministry and then find ourselves struggling for place and power in that ministry. A spiritual debacle! We renounce ourselves to become missionaries and then find ourselves satisfying a subtle self-love by becoming managers of other people's souls in their supposed interests, and by holding on to power when to do so is to weaken the people under us.

The modern application of the man who disfigures his face in order to be seen of men to fast is to make capital out of our little renunciations for human impression. A disease found among the missionaries—thank God, not among all—is self-pity. When we recount how much we have to do, how much we have to give up, and how much responsibility is resting on our shoulders, we are quietly arranging our martyr's crown, unaware, of course, that it may really turn out to be a fool's cap! A man fasting with a long face is not religious, he is ridiculous.

I once watched a man dancing on a raised platform before an idol as an act of devotion to the god. He did exceedingly clever things with his feet, such as standing on the sharp edge of a brass vessel and moving it up the platform while standing on it. As he went through very difficult and very clever performances his eyes were fixed on the idol with a look of devotion, but he was not indifferent to the applause of the multitude. His eyes were on the idol, but his evident desire was that the eyes of the multitude should be on his feet! Very often our very spirituality is a bid for popular approval.

Anoint your head and wash your face, said Jesus, that you may not appear unto men to fast. It is important for religion that Jesus approved the washing of the face and the anointing of the head. The body is to be restrained, but it is not to be treated as an enemy. The Christian Church has not always taken that view. Saint Abraham, the hermit who lived for fifty years after his conversion, rigidly refused from that date to wash either his face or his feet. Saint Euphraxia joined a convent of one hundred and thirty nuns, who never washed their feet and who shuddered at the mention of a bath. "Our fathers," said the Abbott Alexander, mournfully looking back to the past, "never washed their faces, but we frequent the public baths." Saint Athanasius relates with enthusiasm how Saint Anthony, the patriarch of Monachism, had never to extreme old age been guilty of washing his feet. A famous virgin named Silvia, though she was sixty years of age, and though bodily sickness was a consequence of her habits, resolutely refused, on religious principles, to wash any part of her body except her fingers.

All of this is foreign to the mind of Jesus, who

at the very moment that he told them to restrain the body, was careful to imply that the body is to be treated not as an obstacle but as an opportunity.   The difference between modern and medieval society is this: medieval society took the fasting end of the statement as a gospel, turned it into asceticism, and disregarded the statement about the anointing of the head and washing of the face; modern society, on the contrary, takes the anointing of the head and the washing of the face end of the statement as a gospel, and turns it into permanent waves and rouge and lipstick and disregards the restraint part. Between the two there is not much to choose, except æsthetically, for neither of them is Christian.

These words of the poet would express the mind of Jesus:

"Let us not always say, 'Spite of the flesh to-day
   I strove, made head, gained ground upon the whole';
   As the bird wings and sings, let us cry, 'All good things
   Are ours, nor soul helps flesh more now than flesh helps soul.'"

To sum up this first group of three divisions: Jesus said that all this desire to impress through religion is a disturbing symptom of something deeper—the old self-life, once put out but now back again, now dressed up in the habiliments of religion and hence more dangerous and deadly.

The demand of the modern scientific mind for reality and the demand of the modern psychologist for inner integration and inner unity have received from Jesus the most powerful backing. His voice sounds through the ages as the most awful challenge to all veneer, all seeming, all double-mindedness, all unreality in religion.

CHAPTER XIII

INWARD DIVISIONS REGARDING MATERIAL THINGS

AFTER laying bare the three directions in the realm of religion in which we show inner division, Jesus now proceeds to put his finger upon the three divisions we manifest concerning the material. You are not single-minded in your religious life, nor are you single-minded in your material life, said Jesus. And these cross-currents bring collapse. "Lay not up for yourselves treasures upon the earth, where moth and rust doth consume, and where thieves break through and steal: but lay up for yourselves treasures in heaven, where neither moth nor rust doth consume, and where thieves do not break through nor steal: for where thy treasure is there will thy heart be also. . . . No man can serve two masters: for either he will hate the one, and love the other; or else he will hold to one, and despise the other. Ye cannot serve God and mammon. Therefore I say unto you, Be not anxious for your life, what ye shall eat, or what ye shall drink; nor yet for your body, what ye shall put on. Is not the life more than the food, and the body than the raiment? Behold the birds of the heaven, that they sow not, neither do they reap, nor gather into barns; and your heavenly Father feedeth them. Are not ye of much more value than they? And which of you by being anxious can add a cubit to his stature? And why are ye anxious concerning raiment? Consider the lilies of the field how they grow; they toil not, neither do they spin: yet I say unto you that even Solomon in all his glory was not arrayed like one of these. But if God so clothe the grass of the field, which to-day is, and to-morrow is cast into the oven, shall he not much more clothe you, O ye of little faith? Be not therefore anxious, saying, What shall we eat? or, What shall we drink? or, Wherewithal shall we be clothed? For after all these things do the Gentiles seek; for your heavenly Father knoweth that ye have need of all these things. But seek ye first his kingdom and his righteousness; and all these things shall be added unto you. Be not therefore anxious for the morrow: for the morrow will be anxious for itself. Sufficient unto the day is the evil thereof" (chapter 6, verses 19-34). I have purposely left out verses 22, 23 to be treated in the next chapter.

Here we find three specific ways in which we show division in relation to the material.

1. You are endeavoring to lay up in two directions—in heaven and on earth (verses 19-21).

2. You are trying to be loyal in two directions —toward God and toward mammon (verse 24).

3. You are anxious in two directions—the

kingdom of God and the kingdom of physical
wants (verses 25-34).

In other words, Jesus said that we have
no clear-cut philosophy of life toward the
material.

To be able to live a spiritual life in the midst
of a material environment has been and is the
perpetual problem of religion. We alternate between asceticism and worldliness, or else compromise and build up a vast amount of unreality
around religion at this point. As Eucken says:
"In and with all civilization man continues ob-
stinately bent upon the attainment of his own
ends. The struggle for material goods exerts an
immense influence upon and controls man; an in-
describable amount of pretense and hypocrisy
accompanies the spiritual movement."

Most followers of Christ are perplexed because
he seems to take an impossible position toward
the material: "Lay not up for yourselves treasures upon the earth." This seems so very sweep-
ing that it would render the keeping of anything
beyond the actual needs of the day an unchristian thing. It would make it unchristian for the
individual to keep a bank account, to provide for
old age, or for those dependent upon him, or for
an institution to have an endowment. It seems
so impossible and so unworkable that the vast
majority of Christians simply shrug their shoulders, pay a lip homage to it, and then proceed
to live on business policies instead of on Chris-

tian principles. But Jesus did not say, "Lay
not up treasures upon the earth"; what he did
say was, "Lay not up for yourselves treasures
upon the earth." That phrase "for yourselves"
gives the key to the solution of the problem concerning the Christian's attitude toward the material. The prohibition is not against laying up
treasure, but against laying up treasure *for
yourselves.*

Fundamentally, the Christian does not own
anything, not even himself. But he can use the
material to the degree that it makes him more
mentally, spiritually, and physically fit for the
purposes of the kingdom of God. The material
is taken up into his life as a sculptor takes up a
chisel, not as an end in itself, but as a means
toward the end of the perfect statue. The material is not to be looked upon as an evil but as an
anvil, upon which are to be wrought out the purposes of the kingdom of God. The Christian has
but one test in regard to the material: Is this for
myself? Or does it make me more mentally,
spiritually, or physically fit for the purposes of
the kingdom of God? The moment he finds
himself laying up treasure *for himself,* the
moment he discovers a selfish purpose animating
him in the pursuit of the material, that moment
he must let it go or lose his Christian character.
If he finds that he is wanting the material in
order to gain power, to gain prominence, to
satisfy a love of display, to give him selfish ease,

to lay it up without relationship to its use for the purposes of the kingdom of God, he must renounce it or renounce Christ. It is a very delicate moment when a man decides just when the material passes over the line from the purposes of the kingdom of God to the purposes of selfishness, but the Christian conscience must be trained to tell him when that moment comes. The material may be a cog or a clog. As long as it is a cog that fits into the purposes of the kingdom of God he may use it, but the moment it becomes a clog to his spiritual life he must break with it, lest he himself be broken.

We can break the power of the material by its dedication to spiritual ends. In that case the material is no longer the material, for a spiritual purpose runs through it, transforming its character into a spiritual agent. I know a Hindu doctor who, before he operates, takes his instruments and holds them up before a picture of the healing Christ, says a prayer, and then turns to use those instruments in the work of healing. When a man holds up before Christ every power that he possesses, every penny that he has, and says, "These are for thy use, and for thy use alone," then he is not laying up for himself treasure upon earth. He is taking earthly treasure and transforming it into a spiritual agent by holding it up for the purposes of healing of others. The Hindu ascetic tries to be spiritual apart from the material, the real Christian tries to be spiritual through the material. As Suso says, "He who finds the inward in the outward is more spiritual than he who finds the inward in the inward only."

The teaching that a man should give one tenth of his money to God and then be free to use the nine tenths for himself is an utterly dangerous teaching. In giving the one tenth and using the nine tenths for himself he may be buying off his conscience with the one tenth and thereby hallowing an utter selfishness. A rich man was showing some friends through a splendidly appointed hospital that he had built. Everything was up to date and lavish and everyone was in raptures except one man. When the host asked why he was silent, he quietly replied, "If you think this hospital covers the fact of the poor made poorer by your business methods, and that it atones for the grinding of your laborers, then you are mistaken." Very often the giving of the one tenth may be the buying of an indulgence and may be utterly unchristian. The line is not to be drawn at the place of the one tenth, but at the place where our treasure ceases to be laying-up for others and becomes a laying-up for ourselves, hence unchristian. Usually that line will be far beyond the one tenth, but no man can draw that line for another. In the quietness of his own closet he must listen to the verdict of the relentless Voice telling him whether he is living on the

Christian or on the unchristian side of that line.
And he must obey—or perish.

Walker well says, "Our natural love of property is like the thyroid gland. Without it we
are abnormal, but if it becomes too active, we
have spiritual goiter and are choked to death."
They tell us that cancer cells are cells that have
turned selfish, they have ceased to serve the
rest of the body and demand that the rest serve
them. They are no longer contributive, hence
cancerous. Money that has no spiritual purpose
running through its use, that is not dedicated to
spiritual ends, is a cancer, and unless cut out
will eat into the vitals of a man's Christian
character and kill him spiritually.

Whatever gets your attention gets you. If
money, as an end, gets your attention, it gets
you. A villager in India looked through the
window of a dak bungalow (a government rest-
house) and saw a European seated reading before a candle stuck in a whisky bottle. The
villager ran off to his village and announced,
"Now I know what the white man worships—he
worships the whisky bottle, for I saw him burn
a light before it, and he had a book open in
front of it and was saying his prayers to it!"
There is just enough truth in that to make it
sting. But while the modern man is less and
less worshiping the whisky bottle, he is more
and more saying to the Golden Calf of the material, "These be thy gods, O Israel, which brought

thee up out of the land of Egypt." If the modern man doesn't worship the whisky bottle, he comes dangerously near worshiping the golden calf. We scorn the Hindu for worshiping the living cow, but is it any worse than worshiping a dead calf?

Jesus warned us against laying up for ourselves "treasures upon the earth, where moth and rust doth consume, and where thieves break through and steal." Or translated into modern language: "Lay not up for yourselves treasures upon the earth, where falling markets and depreciating bonds doth consume, and where dishonest directors and promoters break through and steal." He was warning not against treasure but the kind of treasure. Some treasure is dead, sordid, subject-to-decay matter; some treasure is alive, for it has a spiritual purpose running through it. It is alive, for it seeks to be alive. It is sacred, not sordid. It is not subject to decay, for it has been transmuted into the gold of the Kingdom by the alchemy of a dedicated purpose. Jesus objects not only to its being without a soul, and hence dead treasure, but he objects also to its being laid up on earth and having no spiritual meaning beyond the present, making it earth-bound. If, however, it is laid up in human personalities, it is coin that is good in both realms. Hence it is living and it is life-giving.

We have one great thing to invest—our lives.

We may invest them in money, making it an end, but if we do, what happens? Money came up out of the earth and it will return to the earth. If our lives are invested in it, they will go to the dust with it. We may invest ourselves in buildings, but buildings came up out of the earth and they will crumble to the earth. If our lives are invested in them, they will go back to the earth with them. We may invest ourselves in physical pleasures, but the body is dust and to dust it will return. If our lives are invested in the physical side of our nature, then they will go to dust with it. The only bank that will not break is the bank of human character. If we invest in people, then our investment is deathless. For you touch people, and they touch others, and they in turn touch others, and on it goes like the ripples of a pond to the utmost shores of eternity. Jesus in the parable of the sower showed how this investing in human character will be very discouraging work, for three out of the four efforts to get a harvest will be lost. Seventy-five per cent of one's investments lost! But one fell on good ground and brought forth thirty, sixty, and a hundredfold. Thirtyfold is three thousand per cent on the investment, sixtyfold is six thousand per cent, and one hundred fold is ten thousand per cent. Large returns! Is it true that if you invest in human personality, you will get back that high percentage on the investment? It is! An almost unknown church-school teacher invested some interest and prayer in a youth named Moody, and Moody, among the hundred thousand that he led into the new life, touched Sherwood Eddy. Among the thousands whom Eddy touched were three youths in India—one became Bishop Azariah, the first Indian Anglican bishop, who is leading the most remarkable mass movement in India to-day; another, K. T. Paul, was for many years head of the Y. M. C. A. in India and the Indian Christian member of the London Round Table Conference; and the third was Santiago, one of the most rarely beautiful Christian souls I have ever known—a Christian statesman. How much percentage did the church-school teacher get out of his investment of time and interest in Moody? Three thousand, six thousand, ten thousand per cent? More than that. He started influences that will never stop.

There is only one place where you can invest life and money and not lose it—in people. Here moth and rust do not consume, and thieves do not break through and steal. Your investment is "safe," and "sound," and "fireproof." I once stayed in a home that had been a Hindu dwelling, but was now rented to a Christian friend of mine. The gods were locked up in the god-room and kept there by the Hindu proprietor. When he opened the room to see how the gods fared, he found that the white ants had been eating them up. White-ant-eaten gods! Many a man will find when all things are opened that his god of money before which he secretly bows is white-ant eaten. It is earth-bound, dead.

Jesus, after warning against the inner divisions regarding the matter of money, goes on and tells how utterly impossible it is to be divided long: "No man can serve two masters: for either he will hate the one, and love the other; or else he will hold to the one, and despise the other. Ye cannot serve God and mammon" (verse 24). He told us unequivocally what we sooner or later find out by experience, that one or the other gets us. The life may be balanced for some time between competing ends, but sooner or later the balance is broken and we go either to one side or the other. The human heart cannot hold within itself two great loyalties. We think we are divided, but that is only outwardly, for in the inner shrine the heart has chosen and the knee has bowed. You sooner or later give your heart to God (the Person), or to mammon (the thing).

A missionary described to me a volcanic eruption and earthquake in the New Hebrides, of which he was an eyewitness. A volcano some miles distant was in eruption and the air was electric with fear that an earthquake would follow. Each laid hold of his most prized possession ready to rush to the seashore to be evacuated in the waiting boats. The expected happened. The whole hill against which the city was built, split wide open. Part of the city was submerged and the sea began to boil. Everybody fled to the shore. As the last boat was about to draw out they yelled to a woman who stood holding a bag of yams to leave the yams and jump into the boat. They could not take both. She stood hesitant for a moment, then refused to give up her yams, and the boat pulled out. They got away just in time, for the land sank into the sea and the last thing they saw was the woman going down under the water, still clinging to her yams. To give the picture a modern setting substitute for the ignorant South Sea Island woman, holding on to her bag of yams, the intelligent business man holding on to his moneybags and letting God and life go. The time comes in every man's life when he has to decide whether there shall be money-dominance or God-dominance in his life. The last we see of many a promising life is its being submerged into a boiling sea of money-interests. He was born a man and died a stockholder, with the emphasis on the "holder."

The imperial coinage of Rome was not allowed within the Jewish temple. Up to the door of the temple it was currency; within, it was not. The heart of the Christian must be an area where the coinage of this world is not currency, where no outside voices rule and only His whisper is law. Jesus in interpreting the parable of the sower said that the heart that represented the thorny ground brought no fruit to perfection because it was choked by "the cares of the world, the deceitfulness of riches, and the lusts of other things." The greatest single factor that keeps men from going on to perfection is the deceitfulness of riches, for no one ever feels that it is a danger to him. A Roman Catholic priest said that he had heard every sin in the catalogue confessed in the confessional, but not the sin of covetousness. Jesus rightly speaks of the deceitfulness of riches, for it deceives the very elect. When he warned the people of this danger "the Pharisees, who were lovers of money, scoffed [lit., "turned up their noses"] at him." Perhaps some of my readers will turn up their noses at this section, will join the Pharisees, will still pray in the temple—and be dead! Or some will take half-hearted steps to break the dominance of money in their lives and end in a compromise. A few weeks ago, going along in a motor car, I saw, on a sign at a tollgate, the word "Halt?"—with a question mark instead of an exclamation point. It wasn't very decisive! Some of us will say to the onrushing dominance of money a feeble "Halt?" but the love of money is so imperious that it does not listen to that kind of command. Every man who desires to be truly Christian must decide to draw a line somewhere in his life and say to money: "Thus far shalt thou go and no further." The sentry of a trained Christian conscience must be on constant guard with a decisive "Halt!" and allow nothing within that cannot give the password, "I serve." Unless money comes to make us more mentally, morally, and spiritually fit for the purposes of the Kingdom we know that it comes not as a servant, but as a master, and in this rôle it does not contribute, it chokes. For Jesus did not say, "Ye must not serve God and mammon," but "Ye *cannot* serve God and mammon"—it is a moral impossibility. We must either serve God with mammon, or try to serve God and mammon, which means only one thing, namely, to serve mammon.

Jesus proceeds in his awful diagnosis of our spiritual difficulties and lays bare our third inner division: You are anxious in two directions—anxious about food and drink and clothing, and along with it anxious about the kingdom of God (verses 25-34). Here anxiety about food and clothing is the dominant anxiety, the anxiety about the kingdom of God is secondary. Jesus would reverse this and make the kingdom of God and his righteousness the dominant anxiety, pledging in that case that the Father will see that you get everything you need in the way of physical sustenance and decent adornment.

Jesus never showed more amazing sanity and balance and yet more incisive penetration than here. Religion has swung between the extremes of Epicureanism—the body as an end, and Ascet-

icism—the body as an enemy. Jesus stops the
pendulum at exactly the right place: the kingdom of God is the supreme value among values,
the body and its desires are to be subjected to
and become the servant of that kingdom, with
the understanding that the servant, the body, is
worthy of its wages and that everything that it
needs is guaranteed. Never were spoken saner
and wiser words. The donkey is a good burden-
bearer. As a ruler it would be hopeless. The
body is a great servant, but as a ruler it makes
life asinine.

Your anxiety-spot is focused all wrong, said
Jesus. You are anxious about what you shall put
on and what you shall put into the body. That
makes the body the master instead of the minister. Shift your anxiety-spot to the kingdom
of God, and the body falls into its rightful position as minister, for in the realm of the Kingdom
it cannot rule. Jesus might have slipped up here
and have done the obvious thing that most of
us would have done, namely, suggest that we do
not pay first attention to the body but to the soul.
Had he done so, he would have transferred our
attention from a physical selfishness to a spiritual selfishness, but selfishness still. Instead of
that he said, "Seek ye first his kingdom [the
new social order], and his righteousness [the new
individual life], and these things shall be added
unto you." He did not shift from physical dominance to a spiritual self-centeredness, but car-

ried us on to the dominance of the kingdom of God and his righteousness, where the body finds its place in service, where the soul finds its place in personal self-realization (his righteousness) and its social self-realization (the kingdom of God). Everything now fits into its proper order and sphere—God, as the Father-King; his Kingdom, as the social self-realization; his righteousness, as the personal self-realization, and the body provided for by all necessary things being added.

Jesus said that all of these anxieties are futile. By taking thought can you add a cubit to your stature? Accept certain limitations—accept your height. You are determined in certain realms, do not fret against them, accept them. But there are other realms open and undetermined. In the realm of the spirit there are no limits this side of perfection. Turn into higher realms all your limited and balked desires. Make your physical limitations a spiritual opportunity. Bunyan, balked by prison walls, turned all his dammed-up energies into *The Pilgrim's Progress.*

All this anxiety about the outer is misplaced and wrong, said Jesus. Consider the lilies of the field how they grow. The emphasis is on "how they grow." You are trying to grow from without in, the real way is from within out. You try to grow by being anxious about food and raiment—these are from the outside; the lilies from within out. Their beauty is the expression of their nature. That is the way God clothes— from within out; you are trying to clothe from without in, and it is a dead failure. It is beauty without a soul, therefore a carcass.

Often the East objects that the gospel has no message for animal creation and that it does not teach kindness to animals. These verses teach that God's loving care and providence extend to the birds and the flowers and that not a sparrow falls to the ground, not merely without the Father's notice, but without the Father being in the very air the sparrow breathes. Animal sacrifice was universal in religion until Jesus became the Divine Self-Sacrifice. Then animal sacrifice stopped wherever he was obeyed, so that Jesus, probably more than any other, saved animal life from senseless sacrifice. Every Christian should show kindness to animals.

Jesus had no maudlin sentimentality, however, about the animal being on an equality with man. He says, "Are ye not of much more value than they?" We are. All life proves it. Animals have in common with us desire for food and for affection, they have some intelligence and seemingly some reason, but they all apparently lack one thing that all men have—a desire for God. As far as we know no animal worships; all men worship, someway, somehow. The animal seems to lack that spiritual nature which makes a man akin to God, that which makes him set up altars of prayer, which makes him long for fellowship with the Father-Spirit. Jesus kept his values straight, for he knew that animals lack something that makes man stand out—"Are ye not of much more value than they?" Human personality is the most precious thing in the universe. If God takes care of the lesser, will he not take care of you, the greater? Then why worry? For worry is the interest we pay on to-morrow's troubles. Worry is distrust, and distrust is sin, so worry is sin against the loving care of the Father.

Jesus' conception of dismissing the yesterdays and not brooding over them with unavailing regrets, of not borrowing troubles from the coming to-morrows, but living as a happy child of God, one day at a time, is beautifully workable. It takes away the impracticalities of brooding over the past and of borrowing from the future, thus saving us from the twin diseases of moodiness and worry and centering us upon the day and its tasks, its opportunities for love and service. This invests each moment with supreme dignity and makes each hour big with destiny.

Jesus never seemed to be in a hurry. He never ran, he never worried. He met each man and each moment as if the whole of eternity were concentrated in that man in that moment. And it was!

CHAPTER XIV

INWARD DIVISIONS IN RELATIONSHIPS TOWARD OTHERS

WE come now to the third and final trinity of divisions in the personality. All three of these concentrate on the outgoings of life. The first set of three had reference to the religious duties toward man, toward God and toward oneself; the second set to our relationships to the material universe and of possessions in particular; this third set has reference to the divisions that occur in our general outlook on life. They are these: (1) The divided outlook (chapter 6, verses 22, 23); (2) The divided out-judgment (chapter 7, verses 1-5); (3) The divided output, verse 6). These all have reference to divisions in the outgoings of life.

Take the first. "The lamp of the body is the eye: if therefore thine eye be single, thy whole body shall be full of light. But if thine eye be evil, thy whole body shall be full of darkness. If therefore the light that is in thee be darkness, how great is the darkness!" The lamp that lights your whole life or makes you grope in darkness is your eye; that is, your eye is your way of looking at things—in other words, your outlook on life. And your way of looking at things will be decided by the question of what you want. What you want determines what you will be. "Desire is king." The lamp of the personality is desire. If thy desire be single, thy whole personality shall be full of light; but if thy desire be divided, then thy whole personality shall be full of darkness. The desire that possesses you takes possession of the will and sooner or later issues in act.

Desire is king! Hannibal at the age of nine years stands beside an altar in Carthage and pledges eternal hatred to Rome, his country's ancient enemy. Years later, when Rome was at his feet, it was but the working out of that concentrated choice. Lincoln stood as a young man in a slave market. As he watched the whole wretched business he turned pale and said to a companion, "I promise before God, if I ever get a chance to hit that thing I will hit it hard." Years went by, and when Lincoln signed the Emancipation Proclamation it was only the unfolding of that permanent choice made years before.

When I was a little boy I saw a picture of a little Hindu boy holding a leopard's cub in his arms and looking at the beholder with a look of inexpressible wistfulness. At the bottom of the picture were the words, "Thirsting for knowledge." I have seen millions of pictures in my life and millions have faded out, but that picture of the little Hindu boy has haunted my years and has been in all my decisions. I see him in all my meetings, and by the look of his upturned face I know that he is still thirsting for knowledge. He makes me weep and he makes me rejoice. At times he is impossible, yet he is always infinitely appealing. I cannot get away from him. I have just paused in my writing to send a cable to China saying I cannot come. I cannot leave the Hindu boy. He will probably haunt all my years. And when I get to the next world I hope to see him again, this time with a glow on his face that tells me he is satisfied with the knowledge of Jesus. The little Hindu boy has hold of me, and in fifteen years of public speaking throughout India I have never missed an appointment or canceled an engagement with him. Desire is king.

I went down into a great city with the Parsee mayor, a man who has transformed a slum city to a city of beauty. When he took me down to the lowest section of the city where his worst problems were, he said to me: "I would do anything for these people if they would only let me, but they won't. They don't want any change. But in the nighttime I wander about these slum parts asking God to help me to do something for them." This single purpose controlling a man has transformed hovels into homes and filth into flowers.

Most of us have no such controlling purpose. We desire many things but nothing supremely.

We are inwardly at clash with ourselves and our inner life powers are neutralized and canceled by conflict. A little girl whom I know intimately was told by her mother to do something. But she was in a petulant, self-centered mood and replied, "I don't want to."

Her mother then said, "Then do this other thing."

Again she replied, "I don't want to."

Then the mother, very busy, said, "All right, then, you do what you want to do."

To which the little girl replied in a rather sad but vexed tone, "I don't want to do what I want to do."

A house divided against itself cannot stand, even if that house be the heart of a little girl.

Jesus sat on the mountainside and looked into the faces of the men before him. He knew that the inner conflict of desires was their difficulty. He knew that to-day Peter would be saying that he was ready to die for him, and that to-morrow he would be cursing and swearing that he never knew him. He knew that Judas would love his Master on one day and on the next day love his money; that the end of the one would be that he would go out and weep bitterly, and the end of the other that he would go out and hang himself. The divided soul ends in mortification, and in extreme cases, in the mortuary.

Principal Jacks startles us by saying in his book, *Religious Perplexities,* that practically all religious perplexities can be resolved by asking one question, "In reference to this thing will I be a hero or a coward?" He insists that all mental perplexities come to us in the shape of a moral choice, that we see with the will. Refuse to make the moral choice, and there is no light. Refuse to step up to the higher road, and the lower road turns to darkness. If thy will be divided, thy whole personality shall be full of darkness. The only way this moral universe will respond to us is by an act of the will. "If any man willeth to do his will, he shall know of the teaching"; he that is willing to do shall know. This was quoted to a wavering Hindu, who thoughtfully replied, "If that is the condition of knowing, then I am afraid I shall never know, for I am not willing to do." His eye was cataracted and his whole body was full of darkness. In this he is not alone, for many of us are straight up against the fact that we are making no progress in our spiritual life, and in our heart of hearts we know where the trouble lies—the unwilling will.

Jesus added an important warning when he suggested that the light within one may become darkness: "If therefore the light that is in thee be darkness, how great is the darkness!" By just a little twist, he said, the good may become bad. That twist has been a bane to religion through the ages.

For instance, the worship of God is light. It

is a beautiful thing, and yet it can so obscure our duty to man that the light becomes darkness.

Service to man is light, but emphasis on service may so shut out fellowship with God and take its place that the light turns to darkness.

The belief in the superiority of the Christian faith is light, but if that belief makes us have a superiority complex toward other races, then that light turns to darkness.

Christian missions are light; they embody a precious sharing of truth and experience and are a beautiful incarnation of service to others, but when they become a system that is foreign, when they sap the spiritual initiative of the recipients by their overlordship and corporationship, when they become ends in themselves and strive to protect themselves instead of creating initiative in others, when they create a mission compound mentality, a mentality that is leaning and helpless, then the light has turned to darkness.

Asceticism is light, for we must renounce on one level to realize on a higher level; but when asceticism assumes forms of physical mutilation, and a means of gaining one's own personal salvation, then it becomes darkness, and how great, in East and West, has been that darkness!

In Hinduism there was the light that men could come into personal communion with God and have oneness with him, but when that light turned into Vedantism with its absorption into the Impersonal and the losing of the human personality, then it became darkness.

Karma is light for it tells us that there is justice at the heart of the universe. But when it was built up into an iron system from which God and forgiveness were excluded, then it became darkness.

Division of labor into the four great divisions: the brain workers, the protectors of society, the traders, and the manual laborers, is light, but when it hardened into the inhuman caste system of India it became darkness, and how great is that darkness!

Buddha was right when he saw that the root of our trouble is desire, but when he tried to root out all desire, even for life itself, instead of replacing the lower desire by a higher desire, then it turned to darkness.

The emphasis on the transitoriness of life is light, for it makes us sit light to earthly things, but when it became the doctrine of Maya— everything a vast illusion—it took away belief in the very reality of earthly living, took away incentive to reform, became a bar to human progress and turned to darkness, and how great is that darkness!

Forgiveness is light—to know that one can find a sympathetic, forgiving Heart in the universe is light, but when forgiveness becomes cheap and easy and is built up into presuming, careless attitudes, or into a system of dispensing forgiveness through priesthoods, then that light turns to darkness, and how great has been that darkness!

Communion of souls in a common faith is light, but when that communion becomes communalism, as it has become in India, where each fights for political rights for religious groups, and where religion becomes a football of communal politics, then that light turns to darkness—and how great, how dense is that darkness!

The sovereignty of God is light, but when it is built up into an autocratic, predestinarian, fatalistic system as it is in Islam, then that light has turned to darkness.

The cross is light, the lightest spot in the universe, but when the cross becomes a mere symbol on churches, or becomes a hard doctrine, or becomes a cheap easy way of salvation which costs us nothing but faith, leaving the essential self untouched, and not demanding that we face life in the same spirit of self-sacrificial giving, then it has turned to darkness. That fatal twist!

So Jesus gives us a double warning: 1. Do not let your eye be cataracted by a double purpose, for the single purpose will flood your whole being with light. 2. Do not let the light that is within you be given a twist so that your virtues become vicious, and your doctrines become deadly.

Jesus puts his finger on another place where we are divided, hence ailing: "Judge not, that ye be not judged. For with what judgment ye judge, ye shall be judged: and with what measure ye mete it shall be measured unto you. And why beholdest thou the mote in thy brother's eye, but considerest not the beam in thine own eye? Or how wilt thou say to thy brother, Let me cast out the mote out of thine eye: and lo, the beam is in thine own eye? Thou hypocrite, cast out first the beam out of thine own eye; and then shalt thou see clearly to cast out the mote out of thy brother's eye" (chapter 7, verses 1-5).

He says that we are divided at the place of our criticisms, or moral judgments. The emphasis of our criticism is on the other man. Center your criticism on yourself, is the demand of Jesus, and the very standard that you set up in your own disciplined life will be the standard by which the other man judges himself. The only possible way of effective criticism of others is by a demonstration of its opposite in one's own moral life.

This sitting in moral judgment on others is the return of the old self-life now clothed in the habiliments of a moral judge. How flattering it is to spiritual pride to be able to dispense condemnation to our brothers, for, by inference, in condemning him we are commending ourselves! When we say, "How bad he is!" we really mean, "How good I am!"

This attitude of censoriousness is always the

sign of a declining spiritual life. We get inwardly out of sorts with ourselves, and then project that upon the other man as an alibi for our own spiritual shortcomings. I have found by actual experience that the moment my own spiritual life sags, in inverse ratio my critical attitudes toward others begin to rise and take possession. Mark Rutherford well says, "If any man is guilty of any deflection from himself, of anything of which he is ashamed, everything which is better becomes a farce to him." The cynicisms of modern youth frighten me, not because I am afraid of their criticism, but because these cynicisms seem a symptom of an inner dissatisfaction with themselves. These cynicisms are the deflected moral judgments of themselves —deflected toward others to save themselves.

Spiritual high temper toward others is usually a sign of spiritual low temperature in ourselves. When religious people begin backsliding, they begin backbiting. The faultfinder hopes by this method that his faults may not be found out. Of course most of this is utterly unconscious, for very few people are consciously hypocritical. Most of those who are, are unctuously so. I do not think that the Pharisee believed for one moment that he was a hypocrite. He had said to himself so often that he thanked God he was not as other men that he came to believe it. That was the deadliness of it, for he was now sincere in his hypocrisy! You may dispense

moral judgments so that by the very dispensing
of them you judge yourself moral.

In a railway train I once took a cup of tea
from a Mohammedan tea-seller who was of doubt-
ful cleanliness. My weariness and a desire for
something to refresh me overcame my reluctance,
but on the cup were these words, "God help you."
I thought them very befitting! I have often wondered whether at many a tea party where people's reputations are being slashed by sharp
tongues, it would not be befitting to inscribe the
cups with some such sentiment in behalf of those
who are absent.

How easy it is to confess other people's sins!
In Travancore the Hindu Maharaja, to expiate
the blood shed in conquering the country, now
feeds the Brahmans and gives them gifts to the
tune of six hundred thousand rupees—all, of
course, out of the state funds, which means out
of the taxpayer's pocket. In the midst of one
of my meetings with several thousand of the
educated there, a Brahman arose and asked me
if I thought it fair to take the taxpayer's money
in British India and pay Christian chaplains. I
replied that I did not think it was fair, any more
than I thought it fair to take the taxpayer's
money in Travancore to feed the Brahmans and
give them gifts costing not less than six hundred
thousand rupees. The audience, made up mostly
of non-Brahmans, howled! But the Brahman
was grieved that I should draw such a parallel

and tried to explain it away. How like the Brahman we are!

An Indian student came to a friend of mine and told him of a new society they had formed, "The Society for the Confession of Sins." My friend was interested in such a novel society and suggested that it must be very difficult to confess their sins to each other in this way. "Oh, no," replied the youth, "it is not difficult, for we don't confess our own sins, but other people's sins." "The Society for the Confession of Other People's Sins" has a very large and, I fear, growing membership throughout the world. But no Christian can belong to it.

This continual sitting in judgment of other people is an abandonment of the love-attitude, hence unchristian. Besides, how do we know all the motives back of the actions and lives of others? I once asked an audience to get together and requested those at the back to come forward. They all came except three people who sat tight. I wondered at their obstinacy and lack of co-operation, but at the close I saw the reason: Two of them were staying with a third who was a helpless cripple, a Roman Catholic, whom they had brought to church for the first time with a great deal of trouble and care. We are too limited, too segmented in our knowledge to judge others. We must leave that to God. He has enough knowledge—and enough love.

If we give ourselves to criticism, criticism will

come back to us with deadly aim. "With what judgment ye judge, ye shall be judged; and with what measure ye mete, it shall be measured unto you." Sow criticism and you will reap criticism, sow love and you reap love. He who would have friends must show himself friendly.

If you habitually take the attitude of criticism, then some day, when life demands of you a positive contribution, you will find yourself bankrupt. I spoke in a packed theater to a great crowd of eager non-Christians. In his closing remarks the chairman of the meeting, an Arya Samajist, head of a college, and a very brilliant man, ripped me and my message to pieces. He was brilliant and sarcastic and cutting. He shone. It was a great triumph, and there wasn't much left of me when he was through. The next night the audience expected me to answer. I arose and said, "You are wondering if there is anything left of me after last night's butchering, but I arise to tell you that there isn't even a bruise. For no one can hurt you from without. You can be hurt only from within. One who tries to hurt another ends in hurting only himself. I find myself utterly unhurt." I then went on with my message. I could leave God and life to answer. Little did I know how quickly they would! The next day we had a Round Table Conference, and, as is our custom, we asked the selected members to share with us what religion meant to them in experience. When it came the turn of this college principal, he began on his usual level of criticism of others, found the atmosphere was not suitable for this, said a few halting things, collapsed and closed. When the situation was demanding something spiritually constructive and something out of experience, he revealed his bankruptcy. God and life had answered, far more potently than I could. They always do answer, somewhere, somehow.

The nemesis is this: When we live on the exhilaration of the wine of the criticism of others, the effect sooner or later wears off, and when we are faced with the demand for something out of our own hearts, then we show our bankruptcy. We have become bankrupt in showing others bankrupt.

Jesus said, cease being divided in your moral judgments. Turn them toward yourself, set up a standard in your own life that shall of itself be a light in the light of which men shall see and judge themselves.

.   .   .   .   .   .

There is one more division upon which, in picturesque language, Jesus puts emphasis: "Give not that which is holy unto the dogs, neither cast your pearls before the swine, lest haply they trample them under their feet, and turn and rend you" (verse 6). The usual interpretation of this saying is that we are not to take the gospel and put it before any and everybody, for not everyone can appreciate it any more than swine can appreciate pearls. They want grain, not pearls.

If this is the interpretation, then it does not fit into anything that has gone before, nor anything that comes after, nor does it seem to fit in with the mind and spirit of Christ. His gospel is open to all, good, bad, and indifferent. But if the meaning is this: That we are not to take the holy thing of personality that is being perfected, and give it to the dogs of desire, nor take the pearl of our spiritual life and cast it before the swine of our lower appetites, lest they trample that holy thing in the mire, and turn and rend the most precious thing we have, namely, our spiritual life— if that is the meaning, then it fits in with what Christ has been saying in his message and it also fits in with the whole of his mind.

His final exhortation about division in character is this: Do not give yourself in two directions. The dogs of desire and the swine of appetite will clamor to be fed at the expense of your highest, at the expense of your spiritual nature. Hold that holy thing, the pearl of a being-perfected personality, high above the heads of the longing swine and dogs of the lower, keep it intact to lay at the feet of Him who redeemed it.

Never was warning more needed, for the moment we begin to divide ourselves between flesh and spirit we find these lower desires to be ravenous beasts which demand more and more, so that we, the real person who might have been perfected into the moral and spiritual image of our Father, are trampled under the feet of beasts and rent to death by them. We must refuse to give to the lower that we may have everything to give to the higher. In the words of the Old Testament: "Take heed to thyself that thou offer not thy burnt offerings in every place thou seest." Save yourself to give a supreme offering of your very all on the altar of the Perfect Life.

THE WAY OUT

CHAPTER XV

THE DIVINE OFFER OF AN ADEQUATE DYNAMIC

In our pilgrimage with the mind of the Master we have come through two great stages: First, perfection as the Father is perfect as the goal, and the unfolding of the meaning and content of that perfection. Second, the diagnosis of the reason why we do not gain that perfection as inward division of motive and character. Never was a more glorious goal set before man—it makes every fiber of one's being tingle at the thought of it; and never was there a more incisive and awful laying bare of our inmost being. We are attracted by the one and appalled by the other. In both cases we are left with a sense of paralysis. Perfection is beautiful, but impossible; inward division is ugly, but actual.

I sat by the bedside of a very dear loved one and we talked about the vacation we would spend together after his operation, which was about to take place. His face lighted up at the prospect and then he sighed and said, "But there is a very deep valley I've got to go through before then." He never got through it. Many of us light up at the prospect of this kind of life, but we know that we must get through that very deep valley of our inner divisions before we can tread these paths to perfection. And many of us fear that we will never get through it.

After watching the fierce and persistent search of the soul of India for inner unity I am prepared to say that it cannot thus be attained. India gives up the struggle and strives, not to unify, but to nullify life. If anyone could do it, India could, but she reduces life to the vegetable and calls it victory. It is a victory that is an utter defeat.

It cannot be done, apart from that which Jesus now proceeds to hold out before us in the way of an adequate dynamic. Without that which follows Jesus holds before us a counsel of perfection which means a counsel of despair. With what follows anything—everything comes within the range of possibilities, nay, actualities. For he now proceeds in the tenderest words to announce the most intimate, the most gracious, and the most utterly adequate offer of the divine coöperation that ever fell upon human ears. Would that it might fall upon our hearts with the same freshness as it fell upon the hearts of those men who sat before him on the mountainside, and would that we might take it with the same abandon as they did! Here is the offer: "Ask, and it shall be given you; seek, and ye shall find; knock, and it shall be opened unto you: for everyone that asketh receiveth; and he that seeketh findeth; and to him that knocketh it shall be opened. Or what man is there of you, who, if his son shall ask him for a loaf, will give him a stone; or if he shall ask for a fish, will give him a serpent? If ye then, being evil, know how to give good gifts unto your children, how much more shall your Father which is in heaven give good things ["the Holy Spirit"—Luke] to them that ask him?" (chapter 7, verses 7-11). In this place I prefer Luke's "the Holy Spirit" rather than Matthew's "good things" as more closely representing the mind of Jesus. I cannot imagine that Jesus, whose coming was specifically to baptize with the Holy Spirit, would lay before us the amazing charter of the new life and then fail to mention the one power that could make the whole possible, namely, the power of the Holy Spirit. It is unthinkable. After all, isn't the difference in the spiritual lives of people just the difference between "good things" and "the Holy Spirit"? Some want "good things" in religion—inspiration, ideals, guidance, forgiveness, and so on—and are content with them, while others are content only with the Holy Spirit, the source of all good things. Some want things, but others are not content with less than a Person. Any spiritual life will be fickle, moody, uncertain, and inadequate that is dependent upon good things coming from without, instead of being dependent on an inner fellowship with a living Person, in whom we have all good things —and more! "Good things" have a way of being transitory, but "He shall abide with you forever." When the rich young ruler ran to Jesus and said, "Good Master, what shall I do to inherit eternal life?" Jesus replied, "Why callest thou me good? None is good save one, even God." He tried to lift the man from the "good thing" to a Person—"none is good save one." For goodness is not possible except we come into vital and immediate contact with the source of goodness— God. Someone has said that "you cannot make up your mind about the good until you have made up your mind about God," which is true. But, deeper, you cannot make your mind good unless you make God's mind your goodness. There must be a transfusing in order to a transformation.

Jesus now provided for the one thing that will make all that he has been saying effective, namely, the inner re-enforcement of our moral natures with immediate and saving contact with the Divine. A righteous but weak will is the tragedy of the world. We are more weak than wicked. And yet that weakness is synonymous with wickedness when there is such a dynamic on the one hand and such a demand on the other. We need life, Life. The prayer of Richard Jeffries is our very own—"Give me life, more life."

"So you think India is turning to Christ?" said a very earnest and able Hindu to me one day. "I am afraid that is very superficial. The men who came out of the meeting last night laughed at your idea that 'religion is a cry for life.' How can the dead understand that? They don't want life, they want to escape from life." That is true of many who have lost their nerve; but most of us have not, and we want life. Religion must manifest itself as victorious vitality or fail humanity. It is reassuring that Jesus now provides for adequate life within, that we may live this glorious life he sets before us.

The coming of the Holy Spirit within means *life*. Jesus in that memorable hour with Nicodemus said, "Except a man be born of water and the Spirit, he cannot enter into the kingdom of God. . . . Marvel not that I said unto thee, Ye must be born from above [margin]. The Spirit breatheth where it listeth [margin], and thou hearest the voice thereof, but knowest not whence it cometh, and whither it goeth: so is everyone that is born of the Spirit" (John 3. 5-8). The figure that Jesus here uses of the Spirit breathing over the chaos of the human heart and bringing to it new life and symmetry and order is the figure used of the first creation: "The earth was without form, and void; and darkness was upon the face of the deep. And the Spirit of God was brooding [margin] upon the face of the waters." Here was a condition akin to that of the human heart before the Spirit brings to it the touch of life. Do not some of us know what it is to have a condition within, that corresponds to that—the inner life without form, and void, and

darkness upon the face of the deep? Without
form! An inner life that is chaotic, no central
purpose running through it, a clash of elemental
forces in the dark. And void! A sense of meaningless futile striving, the hell of getting nowhere, the utter goallessness of life. And darkness upon the face of the deep! We feel that
there are deeps within us unsounded, but darkness broods over them, no sense of certainty
anywhere. And then the Spirit as gently as the
coming of the dawn broods over the chaos of our
inner life, and the miracle, the astounding miracle of spiritual birth takes place. How it is
done we do not know, but we do know that there
is no longer that sense of purposelessness in life,
the void is gone, darkness has given place to
dawn. Just as the Spirit brooded over matter
and brought out of the chaos a cosmos, a world
under the direction of living forces within, moving on to richer unfolding of life, so over the
chaos of our poor lives he broods, and out of it
comes the sense of being taken hold of by life,
by purpose, by power that makes for harmony,
beauty, love. A stark miracle has taken place.
We are born anew! It is futile to argue against
it. Can the unborn argue against the born? The
born know—they live, they move, and they have
their being now in an entirely new world—God.

"You talk about the living Christ within, and
knowing God, and freedom from the old life, and
of being immediately in fellowship with the liv-

ing God. It all gets on my nerves. I don't like it. I go through my religious duties and perform them with care and regularity and yet I know nothing of what you talk about," said a very High Churchman to me one day. And then he added, "And there is father, who is a High Churchman, and yet he talks the same language that you do. You are a very Low Churchman and he is very High, and yet you seem to talk the same language. You are both enigmas to me." Immediately afterward we went into the High-Church service, and as we walked away after it was over he clutched my arm—I thought a little vigorously—and said he wanted to talk with me again. There was a glow in his face as he said: "I know it. It has happened. I opened my heart to Him and it happened. I am a new man." He was! The miracle of the new birth had taken place.

Said an obviously transformed young woman: "I came to India because my husband was called, but I inwardly rebelled, and when I went on board ship I felt I was leaving life behind me in America. But one evening while out walking I found Christ on the Indian road. From that day to this I have felt that I would not mind if he sent me to the loneliest island of the south seas. He is life. I didn't leave life behind me in America. I have it." She too had joined the twice-born.

Jesus uses a phrase that gives us an inkling

of the meaning of this new life: "born from above" [margin]. What does it mean to be born from above? To catch his meaning we must remember that there are five kingdoms representing five stages of life. At the lowest is the Mineral Kingdom, above that the Plant Kingdom, then the Animal Kingdom, above that the Kingdom of Man, and above all is the Kingdom of God. We stand between two kingdoms: the Kingdom of the Animal below us and the Kingdom of God above us. The Kingdom of the Animal stands for a vast self-assertion; war sounds through it; it is "red in tooth and claw"; it stands for the survival of the fittest, for self against all others. Past my window every day go crows holding in their beaks the quivering bodies of young birds robbed from the nests of frantic parent birds. In spite of gleams of altruism a vast selfishness reigns in the lower kingdom. Above us the higher kingdom stands for something different: It stands, not for self against all others, but self for the sake of others; not for the survival of the fittest, but for the revival of the unfit; not for life "red in tooth and claw," but for life crimsoning into sacrifice for the sake of the weak; not for strife, but for harmony, peace, life. Life for us may be born from above or born from below. We may be controlled by the unselfish love of the higher kingdom. How, then, may we pass from the level of mere unregenerate humanity to the higher level of life? To get the clue let us go down to the lowest kingdom, the Mineral Kingdom, and see how it is possible to pass from the Mineral Kingdom to the Kingdom of the Plant. Here on the bosom of the lake is a lotus flower in its white purity. Below it is the foul, polluted mud. They are in two kingdoms and between them a great gulf of purity is fixed. The mud having seen something higher longs to rise and share this higher life. But it cannot will itself there. Nor will education about the higher life suffice, for obviously it needs not information, but transformation. How, then, is it to get up? The way up is the way down. The lotus flower comes down, mingles with the foul earth and says to it: "Would you share my life? Then do two things: renounce your old life of being mud, surrender your life to my life, and utterly trust me." The foul mud does these two things, and up, up, it is lifted above itself and the old life, and, it knows not how, finds itself possessed by new life and blooming in the beauty of the lotus flower. It is born from above. Except the Mineral Kingdom be born from above it cannot see the Kingdom of the Plant. We who are in the Kingdom of Man and are ruled by the selfishness from below are shut up to the same alternative. We cannot lift ourselves into the Kingdom of God however hard we may strive, for if we were able to gain it by our own efforts, then our righteousness would be self-righteousness and that would cut

straight across the very spirit of the new kingdom. Obviously, it is not enough for us to be
educated about the higher life, however useful
education may be. In the words of Doctor Hope
at the Jerusalem Conference: "The world already
knows much of Jesus. We need not only to
know him, but to choose him." Again the way up
is the way down. There is no royal road to God,
but there is a Royal Road from God to man.
God takes it. Jesus, Heaven's Lotus Flower,
comes down, and mingling amid our unclean
world says to us, "Do two things—renounce your
old ways and surrender your life to my life."
Hesitatingly, and often tremblingly, we do it—
for are we not letting go the one thing we have?
But lo, we are taken hold of by power not our
own, infused with life not our own and transformed and transfigured we find ourselves sharing a new kingdom. We are born from above.

This is the first step on the pathway that
leads to the goal of being perfect as the Father
in heaven is perfect. We cannot live life unless
we have life. To get into the kingdom of knowledge we must have intellect, to get into the kingdom of art we must have taste, to get into the
kingdom of God we must have life. The first
step through divided personality is reborn personality. Julian Huxley ends his book by invit-
ing us "to believe in the religion of life." We
do! But not, perhaps, in the way that Huxley
would suggest.

James puts it this way: "Here is a life divided, consciously wrong, inferior and unhappy; that life becomes united, consciously right, superior and happy by its firm hold upon religious realities." A life divided! We have seen in our pilgrimage through this book how painful our inner divisions are. We are at war with ourselves, our spiritual resources exhausted in an inner civil war. Goethe echoed this universal experience when he said, "I find two natures struggling within me." Consciously wrong! No words are emblazoned on the sky declaring our wrongness, but there is that inner sense of having missed the way, of coming out at the place of blankness and futility, and, worse still, of being possessed by a sense of estrangement, of spiritual orphanage—the result of guilt. Inferior! Feeling that we are made for the higher, we live in the lower; made to soar, we crawl in the dust; like a sea-gull, made for the wide ocean and the open sky, spending its days in a mud-puddle in a back yard, so we who are made for God and the perfect life spend our days in mud and muck. Unhappy! Of course, unhappy, for no power on earth can make happy the man who is divided against himself, who is consciously wrong and inferior. It cannot be done. James says that something actually takes place in conversion: the Spirit fuses into one the divided self by the warmth of a new affection; cleanses the springs of life from the biting sense of

wrongness by the gracious offer of cleansing forgiveness; lifts life and makes it superior by the
hallowed sense of having within it the Divine
Guest. As a consequence of all this, life is made
to know the exquisite happiness of inner adjustment, of integration, to know that it shares
something that is eternal, and that God, God,
God is within!

Stanley Hall, the psychologist, is right when
he says that "Every life is stunted unless it receives this metamorphosis in some form or other.
If the church allows this to fossilize, then psychology, when it becomes truly biological, will
preach it, for the chief fact of genetic psychology
is conversion—a fact of unsurpassed scientific
importance and interest." Every life is stunted!
Spiritual dwarfs, moral runts, undeveloped souls
lying in the womb of matter awaiting the touch
of the Spirit to bring them to birth! The Japanese have a way of dwarfing the great forest
trees so they can be kept in small pots. They cut
the taproot so that the tree feeds only on surface
roots, remaining stunted, not higher than a few
feet. Every soul is stunted until it puts its
taproot down into God and begins to draw sustenance from the Divine. If it lives upon the surface roots of a mere intellectual and material life,
it will remain stunted and dwarfed. Spiritual
conversion puts a taproot of faith into God and
there begins a life that draws on Resources not
its own.

Pratt speaks of "this new birth by which a man ceases to be a mere psychological thing or divided self and becomes a unified being with a definite direction." The new man is no longer a mere psychological thing or a divided self, he is a united being with a definite direction— that direction being toward perfection and with power to move on to that goal. How can we move on to that goal unless we have life? Professor Gwatkin says, "We may have philosophy and science, criticism and culture in perfection, and a finely organized society too, and still have no life in us. The spark of life is . . . a true communion with the Divine." I know nothing so necessary in life as life itself.

Lippmann in his honest, and to me, incomplete and pathetic book, *A Preface to Morals,* says that "unregenerate men can only muddle into muddle." He is right. The one thing that the new world awaits to bring it into being is new men. Listen to what a writer on mental hygiene says: "The thousand petty fears and jealousies and prejudices and inhibitions which keep us from perfect harmony and perfect adaptation to persons and conditions that surround us—here is the supreme problem of mental hygiene." It is the supreme problem of mental hygiene and Christ solves it by lifting one above the petty fears and jealousies and prejudices and inhibitions, by lifting the whole tone of the life within so that these things become irrelevant. Canon Raven truly says, "Freed from all self-consciousness, integrated in every fiber of his being, indifferent to praise or blame because free from ambition and fear, taking his place in the community of the universe by his union with God, the new man is far removed alike from the fighting, scheming, advertising, posing self and from the dreaming and ecstasy of the visionary" (*The Creator Spirit*). In the graphic story of the disciples toiling in rowing, with wind against them and making no progress in the dark, it is said that Jesus came to them and that they were afraid and cried out for fear, thinking that he was a ghost. He reassured them and they received him into their boat and—note the point—"immediately the ship was at the land whither they were going." They could get nowhere against the storm, everything was ending in futility until Jesus stepped in—and then, and then they were at the very place they were striving to reach. We are often in that position: we toil in rowing, we strive against the winds of opposition, but everything seems to be against us and we get nowhere. Then Jesus comes to us. We are afraid of him, afraid that he is unnatural, a ghost, asking of us something that is impossible. But we take him in, often reluctantly, and lo, we are at the very land whither we were going and couldn't get there. We have arrived! And it was all so easy when we surrendered to his mind.

To some of my readers this sounds like romanticism. But is it? I stood on the open deck of a ship going down to South America and talked with a very skeptical Latin-American student. He pooh-poohed my idea of God, scoffed at morality, and said that Beauty was the only thing worth while. As we talked I looked up at the sky and said to him, "You see this sky above us—it is filled with music and ideas and thoughts and poetry and facts."

He laughed and said, "Now you are getting romantic and poetic."

"No," I replied, "I am not, for you see that man up in the radio room, he is catching these ideas and thoughts and to-morrow morning what he has caught during the night will be on the bulletin board. He is catching them because he is tuned in to them. You are tuned in to the physical universe alone and deny that there is any other universe, but some of us have tuned in by repentance and self-surrender to the spiritual universe and something has happened; we have caught something, we have been living in a new universe since and on the bulletin board of actual living fact there is the real proof that something has come." The romanticism was fact. "The Spirit breatheth [margin] where he listeth, and thou hearest the voice thereof." The Spirit breathes his regenerating offer through the whole creation, the creation is atingle with the Spirit's healing voice, it throbs in every atom, it speaks in every star, it moves as the central life through all that is, and yet how few tune in and receive the healing Life!

To change the figure, the New Testament speaks of grafting the Divine Life within ours. When that happens nothing is impossible. They tell us that the peach was once used in Persia to tip poison arrows. It is a long way from the peach used to tip poison arrows to the luscious and life-giving California peach, but grafting and cultivation did it. It is a long way from Saint Jerome saying in the fourth century: "I well remember the Scots in Gaul, they were eaters of human flesh," to Henry Drummond the Scotchman expounding and living "the greatest thing in the world"—love. It is a long way, but spiritual grafting and cultivation did it. It is a long cry from the African jungle to Booker T. Washington, but grafting and cultivation did it! It is a long way from the picture we see of the Briton when Servius the Roman said, "The stupidest and the ugliest slaves in the market are those from Britain," to Gladstone the statesman and Christian, but grafting and cultivation did it. It is a long way from the cry that sent terror into the hearts of every plainsman: "The Lushais are coming"—the dreaded head-hunters of Assam—to those same Lushais now coming to the plains to sing the "Hallelujah Chorus," and to sing it exquisitely. It is a long way, but grafting and cultivation did it—and did it in thirty years! I believe in the superman because I believe in the Supernatural Man. That Supernatural Man offers adequate divine resources, and when we take hold of them, nothing is impossible—nothing this side of perfection.

I sat down with one of the finest English characters in India. He had been the head of a local college and for fourteen years had been tutor to two sons of a ruler, one of whom would rule over twenty million people. He told me his spiritual pilgrimage, which was as romantic as a novel. He had come to this very place as a British private soldier, with no education and no ambition for one. But he was converted in a local church, and the conversion meant an awakening of his whole being, including his mind. He resolved to get an education. He walked eight miles each day for a lesson in language. He was laughed at and told that he would not be allowed to take the examinations as they were only for officers. He replied that he would become so proficient that they would have to allow him to take them. He took them! To make a long story short, he became a Fellow of the Madras University, and in the very place where he had been an uneducated Tommy he became the head of the college and a tutor to princes. The secret of it all, he said, was his conversion and the verse he got hold of—a verse which seemed a divine gift to him and which stayed with him during the years: "Behold, I

have set before thee an open door and no man
can shut it." Conversion and that verse made
him. And the end is not yet! To any man who
comes under the sway of the Spirit there is
thrown open a door to endless possibilities. "He
that hath an ear, let him hear what the Spirit
saith" . . . "Behold, I have set before thee
an open door"—an open door out of failure, out
of inner division, out of the old life into victory,
harmony, the new life, and, best of all, an open
door to the life that is perfect as the Father in
heaven is perfect.

The Holy Spirit in this passage in the Sermon on the Mount seems to be an offer not to
make us children by a new birth, but an offer to
those who are already children. The statement
seems to mean: If you are willing to give good
gifts to your children, how much more shall the
Heavenly Father give the Holy Spirit to his
children? Many of us are children, but we have
not come into full possession of the inheritance
that belongs to us as children. I am persuaded
that full inner unity is not usually accomplished by what is known as conversion. It was
not so in my case. I must confess that while
the new life was wonderful, I found that it had
introduced into my life something, which, though
there, was not fully regnant. The fact is that the
introduction of this new life within brought
about inner clashes that I had never before experienced. There seemed to be remnants of the

old life that disputed the right of the new life to rule. This set up friction. This surprising friction sent me again to my Resource for a deeper unity. It came. While it may take ages to attain perfect character, I see no reason why in this life we cannot obtain unity of being by the fusing, purifying fires of the Spirit and a love that may be said to be perfect in that it is perfectly centered on its Lord. Since perfect character is an attainment, it will take ages, but since perfect love is an obtainment, it need not take ages. But it will take the one thing we have—ourselves.

The difference between perfect character and perfect love may be illustrated by the story of the father who came home after a long absence and was welcomed by his little boy with unbounded delight. As the father sat in the house, the little fellow, scarcely able to contain himself with joy, came up to him and eagerly said, "Daddy, can't I do something for you?" The father wishing to respond to the boy's eagerness told him that he might bring him a glass of water. The little fellow, nearly tumbling over himself, ran pell-mell across the room to the water pitcher, poured some in the glass and some on the table, clutched the glass, one little finger in the water, and then ran to his father, the water spilling over the edge of the glass. When he pulled his finger out of the glass there trickled down inside a muddy stream from his not very clean little finger, but the father drank every drop in the glass, while the little fellow stood there rubbing his wet hands on his blouse and saying, "Daddy, can't I do something else for you?" That may not be perfect service, but it is perfect love. Perfect character is a growth, but perfect love is a gift, and that gift can be obtained now—at the cost of our all.

In the fires of Pentecost the discordant elements in the natures of the disciples were fused into one and they obtained what modern teachers call integration. The Spirit lifted them out of themselves and centered their love on a holy Person. The most utterly purifying thing in the world is love for a holy Person. Their love for that Person burned like a lambent flame. We too must undergo that same fusing of the scattered forces of the inner life that our lives may burn with devoted love. "He is a reincarnation of the One Hundred and Twenty," said a Hindu of a devoted Christian. He believed in rebirth and thought the Christian a reincarnation of one of those of the upper room. The impression we usually leave is that we are reincarnations of the disciples in their divided, fumbling pre-Pentecost state. "He speaks as if he is possessed by life," said another Hindu of the same Christian. He was! Unless our gospel can manifest itself as victorious vitality, overriding all obstacles within and without, it will never appeal to this age, an age that desires life.

But we do not lay hold of this offer of Jesus and appropriate it as a working way to live. We occupy ourselves with the marginal, and do not appropriate the central. When the great dam at Assuan, Egypt, was completed—a dam that was to make possible the irrigation system of Egypt—a marvel of skill in the making of it and of usefulness in what it meant to the country, the authorities invited some African chiefs from the interior to visit it. They were taken about the whole dam in motor cars, but they were uninterested until one of them spied a pipe with a faucet on it coming up out of the ground and water flowing from it. They got out of their cars and gathered around it, in high glee over this water-pipe. Not interested in a dam that would send the life-giving waters over the whole of Egypt, but tremendously interested in a water-pipe! Some of us show childish delight in little "blessings," and all the time here is this Central Resource, the mighty overflowing, life-giving Spirit, who would turn our hearts and our society from a desert to a veritable garden of the Lord.

We fail not because our resources fail, but because we fail to link up with them completely. Professor James says that "the brain is probably transmissive, rather than productive." Whether this be true or not, we know that we have little power of productiveness. We run through our resources very quickly. On the other hand, the soul has unlimited powers of transmission. One of the most useful men in India said to me: "I am an electric bulb. I have no light in myself, but God sticks me in here and in there. Sometimes I am a high-powered light and sometimes I am merely a parking light. But I am his and he puts me in where I can serve best." Spencer says that "whatever power an organism expends is the equivalent of whatever power is taken into it from without." This is profoundly true for the Christian. There are men and women of small natural ability who are doing really great things because they are transmissive. They have laid hold of power not their own. The Spirit of God works in and through them. One of the reported sayings of Jesus is, "He that is near me is near the fire," which is true, but not fully true, for if we fulfill his purposes for us, we are not merely near the fire: the fire is in us, the source of our vitality.

A Hindu said to me concerning a certain celebrated sadhu, "He is so wonderful that he can make his pulse-beat stop and become as lifeless as a bit of marble." He expected me to go into raptures. From a psychological point of view it was interesting, but from the point of view of religion it was useless. Do not animals do the same when they hibernate? I want not a lowering of my spiritual pulse-beat, but a heightening of it, till my whole being tingles with God and life.

An inexperienced airman started from Karachi to Bombay. He started late, against the advice of the more experienced, had to travel faster, used up more petrol than if he had gone normally, came down half way with petrol exhausted and wired back, "Forced landing, engine failure." Without petrol, engines usually do fail! Christians do the same when they run out of the Spirit's power. Some of us blame the inefficiency of the gospel when we do not take its Resources. The Chinese have a proverb: "Can a bucketful of water put out the fire of a wagonload of hay?" Can we expect the gospel to do everything for us unless we take everything it has?

How can we take it? The answer is incredibly simple. Jesus says, "Ask, and it shall be given you; seek, and ye shall find; knock, and it shall be opened unto you: for every one that asketh receiveth; and he that seeketh findeth; and to him that knocketh it shall be opened." Never was such carte blanche given to human need. Anyone who has followed Jesus in taking the first step of self-renunciation as he demanded in the first beatitude now has a right—a moral right, to lay hold of the Divine Self for everything he needs. For he now asks, not with his lips, but with his very life. He can now ask with boldness, for he has begun with utter humility, the humility of self-surrender. Dean Inge says that "humility is pure receptivity." Since there is humility there can be receptivity. Ask, seek, knock—the first letters of these three words spell "ask." They all mean the same thing, yet there are degrees of intensity in the words Jesus uses. Some ask, fewer seek, and fewer still knock. I may ask about a man, and that is one degree of intensity; when I seek out the road to his house, it is another; but it is still another when I stand at his door and knock to be admitted to his presence. At the knocking stage I am right up against the problem and there I press my demand for immediate fulfillment. In trying to link up with the Spirit's resources some of us ask, rather feebly in most cases, and leave it at that; others seek with more or less spiritual intensity, but stop short; only those who come face to face with the matter and knock and insist upon knocking until something happens ever find the resources of God thrown open to them.

You may say, "It is not true that everyone that asketh receiveth, for we ask many things of God and we do not receive." Jesus said, "He that asketh receiveth"—not necessarily what he asks; but he receives, if not the thing asked for, then something better, namely, the patience of character that trusts where it cannot see. A little girl in her prayers asked God for something that was beyond the purchasing power of her father. After some days he felt that he should see if her faith had been hurt by no answer from God. So he said to her, "God hasn't answered your prayers, has he?"

"Oh, yes, he has, daddy. He answered, 'No.'"

The little girl was wise since "No" is an answer, sometimes the best answer that God can give, for he says "No" in order to say a higher "Yes" to us.

But this being compelled to say "No" to us is only in the realm of the material. There is one realm in which God does not say "No"—the realm of finding the Spirit. Here everything is open—always! Here we can ask, seek, knock with real assurance. In the tenderest words that ever fell from lips Jesus draws the parallel between the human father and the divine, ending with this great climax, "If ye then, being evil, know how to give good gifts unto your children, how much more shall your Father which is in heaven give the Holy Spirit to them that ask him?" Although you are "evil"—and he puts all in that category—yet you "know how"; it is not merely a spasm of kindliness, it is a groove cut into your very natures. And "if ye then, being evil, know how," then "how much more" shall your Heavenly Father in whose nature is no evil, who gives not as a generous impulse, and who not merely knows how, but, being what he is, cannot do otherwise, for the very expression of his nature is self-giving—how much more shall he give the Holy Spirit to his children?

With these words ringing in our ears it is

strange to find Dean Strong in his Bampton Lectures saying that "the Sermon on the Mount gives no word as to the way of realizing the perfection it preaches; it still remains a law." No word as to the way of realizing the perfection it preaches? Is this offer of the Divine Spirit not an adequate word? Can God give more than himself? When God gives himself, the Divine Spirit, to be the spring of life within us, then does this still remain a law? A law? This is not a law—it is a gospel! The perfect God opens to us the resources of his own nature for the realizing of that perfection; the only thing that keeps us from it is our own imperfect response to this offer. God can offer no more—he can offer no less. Here God's enactments are God's enablements. This is not the piecemeal righteousness of the legalist but the possession of our inmost souls by the Source of Life, and the result is a well of water springing up unto everlasting life.

The only thing that is lacking is the throwing open of every portion of our being to it. The first year I was in India I did not see a drop of rain for six months. The dust was up to one's shoe-tops and the heat suffocating, with the thermometer at 120 degrees in the shade. Oh, for the rains! One night I was sleeping on the roof out under the open heavens when I was awakened by a roar that went up from the bazaar. "Barish a rahi hai," "Barish a rahi hai," "The rains are coming!" was the glad shout that was going up from the sweltering multitudes. The rains had come. Never was anything so welcome. I stood out in it and let it pour over me! And my teardrops mingled with the raindrops. The dust and the heat were over and across the parched ground the very next day was a film of green. The response of nature was instantaneous, for she had been waiting, waiting for this touch that meant life.

One day my soul was awakened by this word of Jesus about the Father's promise of the Spirit to them that ask him. Was I not athirst for his coming? Was not my soul dry and dusty and fretted with the heat of its own conflicting desires? Then I heard the joyful news: "To them that ask"! I could ask—and did. Then the showers, the life-giving healing showers! I opened every portion of my being and let it rain all over me. He had come, and at his touch the desert began to blossom as the rose. Things that I had tended to very patiently by my own efforts and had watched die before my eyes in spite of all I could do, now sprang to life in answer to his touch. My inmost being seemed to be made for just this. This was my life, because it was not my life. Real life had come. And all I had to do was to stand out in it and let it rain all over me!

It was the gift of God.

CHAPTER XVI

HE CALLS TO LIFE

ONE would have thought that after reaching this beautiful climax in the offer of the Holy Spirit Jesus would have stopped there and would have closed his message with the parable of the houses built upon the rock and upon the sand. Why these intervening verses about the Golden Rule, entering the strait gate, and the false prophets? Do they not dissipate the effect of this glorious climax? Could we not stop with the gracious words, "The Holy Spirit to them that ask him" ringing in our ears and hearts? No, for the simple reason that it would have been dangerous to have done so. Religion often suffers from arrested development because it stops at the promises of God, and does not go on to human performances. Any working philosophy of life must *work*. The end is not to see the Resources, but to see them in operation. The work of the Holy Spirit is to produce a holy spirit.

Jesus was a master teacher, so he does the very wise thing of gathering up and laying final emphasis on the outstanding things he has been emphasizing. He epitomizes and lays final emphasis on three things:

1. A comprehensive principle of guidance in

regard to reverence for personality: Do unto others as you would that they should do to you (verse 12).

2. A final plea for self-realization through self-renunciation: Enter ye by the narrow gate, . . . for narrow is the gate that leadeth unto life (verses 13, 14).

3. A final warning against double-mindedness and spiritual unreality: Wolf in sheep's clothing (verse 15), grapes of thorns and figs of thistles (verse 16), good tree and evil fruit and bad tree and good fruit (verses 17-20), followers of his who cast out devils in his name but have not cast out the old life from within (verses 22, 23).

The reader will recognize in these cryptic and epitomized sayings the outstanding notes which Jesus had been sounding through the whole of his Message on the Mount. The three notes are: Reverence for personality, Renunciation of spirit, and Reality of life. He knew how quick we would be to fly away on the wings of the mystical note he had sounded about the Spirit, so he calls us back to the three stern realities: in reference to our brother's personality we are to be reverent, in regard to our own we are to be renounced and real. The fact is that these verses sum up quite exhaustively what he has been saying throughout the Sermon. Even the note of perfection is not absent, since he said that the narrow road of self-renunciation "leadeth unto life," and "life" in the broad and final sense here used is synonymous with perfection.

Our duty toward our fellow man is summed up in what is called the Golden Rule. But this is really not a "rule," for Jesus never gave rules of life. It should be called the Golden Principle. Rules are soon outgrown, for they are made to fit local situations, which rapidly change. Since principles are the same yesterday, to-day, and forever, they are never outgrown. We make rules out of principles, to fit changing situations. The rules change but the principles do not. In a religion founded on rules, such as Islam, one of two things happens : either the people in growing break the rules or the rules are so strong they break the people. Jesus therefore wisely gave no rules of life, but he did give principles, which are capable of living amid changing and advancing civilization and are never outgrown. This Golden Principle is one of them. We are to treat others as we would like to be treated were we in their place. That principle will never be outgrown either in heaven or on earth. No wonder many Hindus at our Round Table Conferences say that their religion is "to do unto others as they would like others to do unto them," often quite unconscious that it is from the gospel. But Jesus did not say this was new. In fact, he said that it was the essence of the Law and the Prophets. If it is the essence of the Law and the Prophets, it took a Divine Mind to distill it. The

new thing is not merely that it is positive, while
the same principle among the Chinese is nega-
tive. The new thing is in its content. Raphael
and the veriest dauber use the same paint and
the same colors, but the new thing is the content. For into this verse is poured the content
of the whole of that part of the Sermon on the
Mount that refers to human relationships, or, as
we have called it here, reverence for human personality. The word "therefore" in this verse
gathers up everything that he has been saying on
this subject. The cream has risen up in this
verse from the milk of the whole of the preceding Sermon. This verse means that we are to
treat those socially and economically below
us, those who are contemptuous toward us in
smiting our cheeks, and those who are our
enemies, as we would like to be treated were we
in their place.

This takes imagination, large-heartedness, and
large-mindedness. To see the other man's view-
point, to enter into his feelings, to project oneself into his situation—this requires just what
Jesus has been insisting upon, namely, that the
tyranny of the self-life must be shattered in order
that we may have an inner life sufficiently free
from itself to enable us to project ourselves into
the pains and sorrows and difficulties of others.
When Ezekiel went to the captives by the river,
he went "in the heat and bitterness" of his spirit.
He would lay down the law of God to them!

But God said to him: "No, Ezekiel, not yet. Sit down with them and learn what they have to go through with." And "for seven days I sat where they sat." For seven days he learned sympathy. At the close of the seven days God said to him, "Now, you may speak." Now he could speak, for he knew! If we could only sit where people sit, if we could only put ourselves in the other person's place, what a difference it would make in our actions toward them!

God acts on this principle. In Jesus he has sat where we sit, has been subjected to the same limitations, the same temptations, the same tortures that wring our hearts. Our God knows. Not from the scrutiny of heaven, but from the sufferings of earth. He puts himself in the other person's place. He treats men as he would like to be treated if he were man and we were God. There is no blasphemy, but a recognition of this fact in the plaintive words on the tombstone:

> "Here lies Martin Elginburgh;
> Have mercy on his soul, O God,
> As I would do, were I Lord God
> And ye were Martin Elginburgh."

What a difference it would make in our economic system if the employer would treat every employee as he would like to be treated as an employee, if he would give every girl the wage he would like his daughter to have were she an employee; in our race relationships if we treated the

Negro and other colored races as we would like to be treated if we were colored.

The Hindu Vedantist, believing that everything is just the One, says that his principle is deeper than this Golden Principle in that the other person is your very self, so you are to act toward him as you would like to be acted toward, for in that case you act toward yourself in the other person. I cannot help wondering if this is not still selfishness, though refined and religious and seemingly highly spiritual. If I love myself in the other man, I am still loving myself, however refined and spiritual it may be.

Jesus lays down something that deepens the conception of treating others as we would like to be treated, when, in depicting the Last Day, he said, "I was an hungered, and you gave me meat" (Matthew 25. 35), and when, in answer to the puzzled question of the righteous as to when they had seen him in that position and had acted thus toward him, he replied in these remarkable words, "Inasmuch as ye have done it unto one of the least of these my brethren, ye have done it unto me." To feed the hungry is to feed the Lord who hungers in the hunger of that man. To visit the sick is to visit Him who suffers in the suffering of the sufferer. This puts into the treatment of others, not merely a humanitarian motive but a deeply religious one. It combines these two streams into one. In treating other persons as you do, you really treat the Lord of your heart in that way, for the Son of man is identified with the sons of men in the perpetual incarnation of human need. There is an ancient saying, "When thou seest thy brother, thou seest thy Lord." In thus identifying himself with human need Jesus deepens the conception of our duty toward others, and at the same time saves us from the refined selfishness of loving our own self in the other person. For in this conception we do not love ourselves, but our Lord in the other person. Love of oneself even in the other person is selfishness, but the love of the Other in the other person is love.

In the medieval days, when the gospel of Christ was perverted and men sought selfish power through religion, pious monks were especially warned against two classes—"bishops and women." That all bishops should not have been included in that class may be seen from this beautiful and very Christian story: When the Roman army had captured, but refused to support, seven thousand Persian prisoners, Acacius, Bishop of Amida, undeterred by the bitter hostility of the Persians to Christianity, and declaring that "God had no need of plates and dishes," sold all the rich church ornaments of his diocese, rescued the unbelieving prisoners, and sent them back unharmed to their king. I think I hear the Master saying to the good Bishop, "Inasmuch as ye have done it unto these, my brethren, ye have done it unto me."

In summing up all that he meant by reverence for personality one does not see how Jesus could have expressed it in fewer words nor in a more telling way than in this Golden Principle.

.   .   .   .

Jesus now goes on and sums up all that he has been saying on being renounced in spirit as the first step toward "life," or perfection, in these words: "Enter ye in by the narrow gate: for wide is the gate, and broad the way, that leadeth to destruction, and many be they that enter in thereby. For narrow is the gate, and straitened the way, that leadeth unto life, and few be they that find it" (verses 13, 14).

The usual interpretation of this verse is that the gate into heaven is very narrow and few are going to get in. But Jesus says nothing about heaven. He says that the way to find "life" is by a narrow gate. It brings back the same principle we have been enunciating again and again: the way of self-realization is by way of self-renunciation. This is saying in pictorial language what he said in that passage—which, by the way, is the most oft-repeated passage in the Gospels— which shows incidentally how much emphasis Jesus placed on it: "Whosoever would save his life shall lose it: and whosoever shall lose his life for my sake shall find it." This is the very heart of his philosophy of life, and it would be amazing if he did not repeat it here in other language. What he seemed to mean was this:

Center yourself on yourself and you will find yourself disintegrating, lost; lose yourself in some cause, or some person outside yourself and you will find yourself coming back to you, realized, found. There is no blinking of the fact that this cuts straight across practically the whole of the underlying philosophy of Western life, with its self-assertions, its self-advertisements and its competitions, to say nothing of its wars. That underlying philosophy says that the self must not be denied—it must be expressed. Anything else is narrowness, and we loathe narrowness. The underlying strain in Christendom is between these two ways of thinking. Which way brings us to "life"? Is Jesus' way of finding life by losing it an unnatural, imposed and strained way of living, or does it come up out of the facts of life?

Is it true physically that the way to find physical freedom and power is by a narrow gate? Here are two young men who have two diametrically opposite views on the matter. One says that he is free to do as he likes with his physical body; he eats when and what and as much as he wants; he indulges his sexual appetites as he desires; he says that he has a right to taste all experience. He is physically free. But here is another young man who, having an ambition to be an athlete, restrains his physical appetites; keeps under his sexual impulses or sublimates them into higher forms of creative activity;

goes through a very strict regime of disciplined training. He is not free—he is bound by the laws that underlie physical life. The field day comes, in which these two ways are to be tested under the real test—the test of life. These two young men enter the same event. At the crack of the pistol they are off, but half way to the goal the first young man is winded, is falling steadily behind, beaten, while the other rhythmically and masterfully pulls out from the rest and crosses the line an easy winner. I come to him and say: "You have physical life and freedom—how did you get it?"

He thinks back over the years of obedience to physical law and says: "This way is narrow. I got it through a narrow gate."

The other young man tried to gain physical life through a broad gate, and he found in the crisis that it would not open to him. It shut its door in his face and said, "I never knew you."

Is this law true in regard to the life of the mind? Here are two young men who hold opposite views about the way to find mental freedom and life. One says that he is free to do with his mind as he likes. He listens to lectures when he desires, he makes no discrimination in his reading—his whims decide; he carries on conversations long after they have run out of intelligence —he is mentally free. The other young man is not free: he gathers up his spare moments and makes them contribute to his central purpose;

he discriminates in his reading, knowing that if he reads this book he cannot read that; he puts himself under a strict mental regime. The examination day comes when these two ways of life are to be tested. The first young man enters the examination hall hoping that luck will be kindly, but in ten minutes he has run out of intelligence, his mind becomes more and more confused, beads of perspiration stand out on his forehead. As I watch him I say to myself, "But I thought you were mentally free—you don't look it now!" The other young man looks at the paper and smiles. He writes and writes, for all the sages of all the ages seem to be at his command and offering their tribute of wisdom and learning. He does it easily and masterfully, and the results show him to be at the top of the class. I come to him and say, "You have mental life. How did you get this freedom?" He thinks of the years of discipline and says, "This way is narrow. I entered by a narrow gate."

The other young man trying to enter by a broad road found in the crisis that he had only mental bondage.

Take the realm of harmony. Listening to a Kreisler one feels the sense of ease and mastery with which he plays. He seems to be at home in the realm of harmony, it is all so natural and unstrained. I go to him and I say, "You have freedom and life in the realm of harmony. How did you get it?"

He recalls the years when he put himself more and more under the laws of harmony, became their obedient slave, set up higher and higher standards, became more and more self-exacting, and then finally burst into creative freedom. He very thoughtfully replies: "This way is narrow. I entered by a narrow gate."

But suppose I should say to myself, "I don't believe in all these laws of harmony, I believe in being free." So I bang on any note on the piano I like—I am practicing self-expression in music! I may be free to do this, but you would not be disposed to sit and listen. I cannot practice musical self-expression until I have by self-surrender to musical laws created a musical self to express. A great many people talk about self-expression who have no self to express. They have inward chaos and call it a self. No one can express himself until, by losing it, he has found a self to express.

Take the realm of art. Here is a group of people standing before a masterpiece in an art gallery. Something has gone into that picture, for something is coming out of it that holds that group in its grip. I come to the artist and say, "You have found creative freedom in art. How did you get it?"

He tells of his obedience to the laws of coloring and conception, of how he put himself more and more under their sway until they became identified with his inmost being, and then how he rose to freedom, and adds, "But this way is narrow."

But suppose I should say, "I believe in being free," and in the name of freedom should disregard all these laws and should daub as I like. No one would stand in front of my picture. Nothing has gone into it, so nothing comes out of it. I tried to get into art by a broad road and it would not open.

If this is true in other realms, it is more deeply true in the realm of the moral and the spiritual. Knock at the doors to life as you may, in the end, if you want to find life, you must find it by the narrow door of self-losing. This law holds good for God as well as man. If Jesus is the human life of God, then, in the cross, he shows that God too takes this way. Jesus could say, "I am the Life," because he went through the narrowest of narrow doors of self-losing. For God, for Christ, for man, this law holds good. It is written not merely in the pages of the Bible, it is written in the constitution and make-up of the universe. It is a spiritual law which is as inescapable as the physical law of gravitation.

Jesus, knowing that the supreme issue of all human living is involved, namely, the finding of life itself, and knowing that we would take all that he has been saying as something to be looked up to but not to be sought and found, makes a penetrating appeal, saying, "Enter ye in by the

narrow gate. . . . For narrow is the gate
. . . that leadeth unto life."

.   .   .   .

We come now to the last of the three things in
which he recapitulates the whole Sermon. These
three things may be summed up in the three
words, "Do" (verse 12), "Enter" (verse 13),
"Beware" (verse 15). In religion there are
things which we must do unto others, things
which we must enter for ourselves, and things of
which we must beware. The third grows out of
the other two. What was the final and supreme
danger of which he solemnly warned them? It
was twofold: First, that they would try to *do*
what he had been saying, without *being* what he
invited them to be. They would try to do unto
others, without entering into life for themselves.
"Beware of false prophets, which come to you in
sheep's clothing, but inwardly are ravening
wolves. By their fruits ye shall know them. Do
men gather grapes of thorns, or figs of thistles?
Even so every good tree bringeth forth good
fruit; but the corrupt tree bringeth forth evil
fruit. A good tree cannot bring forth evil fruit.
. . . Every tree that bringeth not forth good
fruit is hewn down and cast into the fire. Therefore by their fruits ye shall know them" (verses
15-21). Just what is the essence of that which he
is warning against in these verses? It is this:
You will try to impose these things that I have
been saying to you on the framework of the old

leaving the old as it is with these things added.
So you will have sheep's clothing on wolf nature,
grapes on thorns, figs on thistles, good fruit on a
corrupt tree. Jesus saw the supreme danger, that
men would take what he was saying as the imposition of a new code, instead of the offer of a
new character. This would result in a hodge-
podge of a new code on old character. The
whole thing would be unnatural, strained, and
impossible—as impossible as finding grapes on
thorns, or figs on thistles, or good fruit on a bad
tree. Luke in a parallel passage makes the issue
very clear: "The good man out of the good treasure of his heart bringeth forth that which is
good; and the evil man out of the evil treasure
bringeth forth that which is evil: for out of the
abundance of the heart his mouth speaketh"
(Luke 6. 45). His way of life was to be the overflow of the heart, or, to change the figure, the
natural flowering of good hearts into good deeds.
Their piety was to be as natural, as unstrained,
as overflowing, as gracious as his. His came
from the depths; theirs must also. He knew
that the tragedy would be that they would build
up what he was saying into a code and leave the
depths untouched. They would take these words
of his as regulation for conduct instead of as a
regeneration of character. But Jesus is not
primarily a sage, he is a Saviour. The Sermon
on the Mount cannot be lived apart from the
Saviour on the Mount. And this Saviour comes

not to save us from doing bad deeds to doing good deeds, but to save us from being bad men to being good men.

It is strange, and yet not strange, that Jesus' anxiety about spiritual reality is different from ours. We are always telling people that they must *do,* lest they be hypocritical, while Jesus was always insisting that people *be,* lest they be unreal. We are anxious about the kind of *deed;* Jesus was anxious about the kind of *person.* He was interested in good men who would flower into good deeds.

In the first part of this book I mentioned the healing of the deaf and dumb man, with the crowd saying that, "He hath done all things well: he maketh the deaf to hear, and the dumb to speak." In the midst of it Jesus "sighed." Why? The reason was that they would interpret the "all things well" as making "the deaf to hear, and the dumb to speak," and would leave it at that—and be content. He came to do something infinitely deeper and greater than that, but they took the surface thing, the little thing, and let the deeper and greater thing go. The good that he was doing was blocking the best. No wonder he sighed. I can hear that same sigh in these closing words of the Sermon on the Mount: "They will take my sayings and impose them on the old life. They will muddle things badly, find the whole thing impossible and let it go as unworkable. They will not let me do the thing I have come to do—make them new. They will part my garments of thought and idea among themselves, and wear them as Christians, but they will leave me tortured on the cross of their old untouched lives.

Jesus' final appeal is that we make the tree good that the fruit may be good. Be good at the depths that you may be good at the surface. But I hear you say: "It is impossible for the tree to change its nature. If it is not good, it is not, and nothing can change it." But remember the peach and the graft! Christ grafted into the inner life makes Christlike living possible, yea, the only natural thing. "Christ in you—the hope of glory"—the hope of the glory of that perfection which he holds out before us.

"Christ is in my lifeblood," said a radiant Christian at one of our Round Table Conferences. And that is where Christ wants to be. There "he is able to save us to the uttermost." He is able to save to the uttermost, but in no lesser way. If he is to be the Saviour of life, he must be the source of life.

How amazingly thorough and realistic this Man is! He has just laid on us the most amazing program ever laid on human beings, and yet he is not satisfied with an obedience to it that does not spring from the sources of life itself. He would be in our lifeblood, as well as in our life-work.

That would be thorough enough, we should

think, but he goes on and speaks to one more possible unreality, namely, that of saying that Christ is in our lifeblood and leaving it at that. No, said Jesus, the test of the inner life is its manifestation: "By their fruits ye shall know them."

Here he lays down a searching and scientific principle of judging. Had this Voice come out of the halls of a modern university it could not have been more up to date. The dictum of modern thinking is this: "The outcome is the criterion." You cannot tell whether a thing is true until you put it under life to get its verdict. "In any battle of ideas victory will go to those ideas that are guaranteed by the facts."

As followers of Christ we are willing to submit Christ and his gospel to the test of fruit. Wherever it is seriously tried it works, and works to the degree that it is tried. I was asked to speak before a university which is the home of the mechanistic psychologists. The subject they asked me to take was "My personal religious experience." Now, the last place on earth in which I would want to bare my soul would be before mechanistic psychologists. But they asked me, and I felt that not I, but my Master and his gospel were on trial. I unfolded as simply as I could what he meant to me. For over an hour they gave me a very patient and, I thought, sympathetic hearing. But at the close a man arose and said, "Isn't it possible that you are suffering from an hallucination?"

"Yes," I replied, "it is possible, for others have suffered from hallucinations, and I am not proof against them. But if I am, then it is in spite of the attitude I have taken these years, for I have taken my faith and have put it out before the non-Christians and skeptics of the world and have said, 'There it is, brothers, break it if it can be broken.' But I can honestly say that the more it has been smitten on the more it has shone. Besides, if it is an hallucination, it is a life-giving hallucination, for it has given me exactly what I need, so that it has done me more good than my former sanity."

The crowd applauded. The man looked around in surprise and was heard to say, "Well, it looks as though I am in a minority here to-night." He was! For men in spite of being psychologists remain persons, and cannot escape the voice of the supreme Person. His gospel works!

And now there is nothing left, but for us to work it. He sends us away with these words ringing in our ears: "Not everyone that saith unto me, Lord, Lord, shall enter into the kingdom of heaven; but he that doeth the will of my Father which is in heaven." We have explored his mind, we must now express it. A Hindu lady, gracious and winsome, ended her chairman's remarks in one of my meetings with words that are not only interesting, but expressive of many a tendency: "After this address to-night I do not think we should have questions. We should go home and dream and dream." Jesus knew how easy it would be to go away after hearing his words and "dream and dream," so his last words to us are that we should go down from the Mount and do and do.

CHAPTER XVII

THIS LIFE HAS SURVIVAL VALUE

JESUS now enforces his message and gives weight to the issues involved by a simple, but striking parable of the two men who built their houses, one on sand and the other on rock: "Everyone therefore which heareth these words of mine, and doeth them, shall be likened unto a wise man, which built his house upon the rock: and the rain descended, and the floods came, and the winds blew, and beat upon that house; and it fell not: for it was founded upon the rock. And everyone that heareth these words of mine, and doeth them not, shall be likened unto a foolish man, which built his house upon the sand: and the rain descended, and the floods came, and the winds blew, and smote upon that house; and it fell: and great was the fall thereof" (chapter 7, verses 24-27).

In choosing the substance that would best symbolize the solidity and substantiality of his teaching Jesus chose a rock. But is not this symbol of the rock incongruous? Has he not taken away the really substantial things and left us with airy ideals that are anything but substantial? He has startled us with the daring of his message and now he further startles us by this word about its finality. What he says is this: "Try all the ways of life you may, and in the end you will find that nothing comes out as solid reality but this way of mine. Everything else is sand; this way is rock." This is breathtaking—is it true?

The first three beatitudes with their insistence on renunciation in spirit, the calling of those happy who suffer vicariously for others, and who thus become the meek who are said to inherit the earth—is this rock? Rather does it not seem that the self-assertive, the selfish and the proud constitute the rock? Consider their self-sufficiency, their hardness, and their strength—they are the stuff out of which empires are made! Made—or wrecked? Napoleon stands as the sum total of the spirit of self-assertiveness. Could any one have made this spirit succeed, he could. Did he? In the beginning it did seem to work, for Europe was at his feet. But in the end? The beginning of the end was when he met the soft, gentle snows on the road to Moscow. What could snowflakes do against the hardness of his spirit? They broke him. They symbolize the breaking of this man of iron and blood and selfishness by the gentle imponderables. The fitting and only end of that type of life is the isolation of Saint Helena, where amid tinseled loneliness he sat. His rock had crumbled to sand. And when the French nation voted on the question of who was the greatest Frenchman they passed by this man of self-assertion, whose selfishness led to the butchery of millions, and chose Pasteur, the man of self-dedication, whose service has saved the lives of millions. In doing so they unconsciously pronounced their judgment that the way of the self-dedicated, serving meek is rock. This type is slowly but surely coming to the inheritance of the earth. They are the fittest to survive.

Are those who hunger and thirst after righteousness, who are merciful toward others and thus become the pure in heart that see God—are these rock? Righteousness, mercifulness, purity of heart—how unrocklike they seem alongside the hardness of unrighteousness that cares nothing for moral distinctions, that has no mercy toward the weak, and that obeys the impulses of passion rather than the law of purity! But only at first sight are they rock. Try to build society on rejection of righteousness, on unmercifulness toward others, on disregard of sexual purity, and what happens? That society is bound to fall by its own rottenness. Sin is suicide, both for nations and for individuals. The soul is made for righteousness, for mercifulness, and for purity of heart as the plant is made for sunlight, as the fish is made for water.

The persecuted, but joyous peacemakers—are they rock? Are they the anvils that wear out the hammers of the persecutors? Call the roll in history and every single idea or person that to-day is dominant, and that is beneficent in its dominance, was once a persecuted idea or person. How rocklike seemed the persecutors, and how like sand seemed the persecuted. But though one generation stoned them, the next generation took part of those stones and built a monument to the persecuted. Beneath the rest of the stones lie the persecutors rotting, forgotten.

To gather up values in the past and fulfill rather than to destroy seems so unsubstantial alongside the quick, easy, seemingly sure way of the iconoclast. Tear down everything, start all over again—how rocklike that seems! In a procession in Calcutta, formed for a single purpose, were two banners, "Up with Revolution!" and "Down with Revolution!" It didn't matter whether it was "up" or "down," just so it was "revolution." This was not the mind of Jesus. He knew what we are just learning, namely, that he who disregards the past will find the future disregarding him. He only lands safely into the future who leaps from the springboard of past achievement and discovered truth. This demands patience and sympathy, but in the end it turns out to be rock and it stands, while the quick, impatient method of iconoclasm turns out to be sand. Revolution gave it birth, revulsion kills it.

Contempt for others, the power to wither them with look or word—how hard and strong that seems! Reverence for personality—how soft and weak! The hardness of the one is so hard that it is brittle, while the softness of the other turns out to be the softness of the tiny root that rends the mighty rock. General Dyer's "crawling order," when he made the Indians that went along a certain street crawl on their stomachs in expiation of having knocked down an English woman, seems strong and rocklike, so much so that many hastened to call General Dyer "the saviour of the Punjab." But this contempt for others soon revealed how sandlike it was, for events quickly showed General Dyer to be "the loser of India." India was lost to Britain for twelve years after Dyer; and if she is regained, the reverence for personality that Lord Irwin and others like him have shown will be responsible. Contempt for the person and rights of the laborer has nearly wrecked capitalistic society. It is being saved only where contempt is giving way to respect and appreciation and the granting of human rights. One, seemingly strong, has turned out to be sand; the other, seemingly weak, has turned out to be rock.

To march to court with your adversary, to overawe him with clever legal talent, to try to crush him with courtroom processes and tactics —how strong and invincible it seems! And how weak and humiliating it seems to meet the adversary in the way and to strive to come to an agreement with him by reason and willingness to see his side. Yet the method of crushing an adversary in court soon shows its weakness, for both begin to realize that they have put their feet into flypaper and the more they struggle the more enmeshed they become. The one method leads to "the utmost farthing," the other to the utmost friendliness.

To take toward woman the attitude that she exists for the gratification of man's sexual passions and to be able to divorce her at will appears strong and rocklike. To treat her as an end in herself, to make her one's equal in the marriage relation—this seems weak, so much so that when this was announced to the disciples they said in dismay, "In that case it is better for a man not to marry." But when these two ways are put under the test of life what is the verdict? In Moslem lands one method has been tried: the home has become the harem, woman has become the object of sex, divorce at the will of the man. The result? Every land where Islam has gone has become a waste-land. The Moslem man is involved most deeply in the general decay. "Our religion is gone, and the general backwardness of our people is responsible for it," said a Moslem prime minister to me. Islam has founded its house upon the sand of unequal treatment of woman, and if we cannot say, "Great is the fall thereof," the facts do allow us to say, "Great is the decay thereof," and the end is the same.

How rocklike seems the multiplication of oaths in our affirmations, with what force and power do they come; and how sandlike seems the simple straightforward speech of Yea, yea, and Nay, nay. Yet the piling of oath on oath begets the impression that "we do protest too much." Instead of ending in confidence, it ends in collapse. The man who in simple, straightforward speech builds up a reputation for utter sincerity —how rocklike he finally becomes! On such characters nations are built.

"An eye for an eye and a tooth for a tooth"—how obvious and sensible and strong that principle seems! Could anything be more obviously rock than this? And the turning of the other cheek, the going the second mile, and the giving the cloak also, could anything be more obviously sand than this? But when we apply it to life, what happens? The outstanding Moslem leader in India to-day recently saw in a train a Christian reading his New Testament and turning to him said: "Your religion is too tame for us. We believe in an eye for an eye and a tooth for a tooth." Scarcely were these words uttered when three hundred dead lay in the streets of Cawnpore as the result of Hindu-Moslem riots. The result of the application of this doctrine to life, whether applied by Moslem, Hindu, or Christian in East or West, is ever the same. Lathi for lathi, blow for blow, eye for eye, tooth for tooth—the leaping flames of burning houses and the groans of the dying are the eloquent comment on this doctrine applied to life. But this is not the worst result. Doors to political and social advance have been thrown open before India—can she enter? She is kept from entering only by the spirit of suspicion and retaliation and the clash between Hindu and Moslem. India became great when she conquered by turning the other cheek, she is now becoming small as her sons smite each other's cheeks. And this leader and his co-religionists must know the tameness of being governed from the West, because he thinks it "too tame" to go beyond the letter of the law to bring about agreement and reconciliation. One seems like rock and in reality is sand, while the other seems like sand and in reality is rock.

The method of getting rid of your enemies by loving them—how unsubstantial it seems alongside the quick, solid way of getting rid of them by force! But the method of force turns out to be the great illusion, for if you conquer the body of a man you do not touch the real man. He is still an enemy and now a worse enemy than ever. You have conquered his body, but not his soul. Only love and good will are strong enough to reach down to the inner life and turn one from enmity to good will.

With what rocklike strength strode the men into the room in Vienna to send the ultimatum to Servia, its terms so impossible that war was inevitable. After the war I went into that same room and saw a scene of confusion—the chairs were topsy-turvy, the pictures were off the walls, the carpets were rolled up—all of this a symbol of the chaos, the unutterable chaos that the introduction of this principle of force had brought into Europe. The house of Europe—not Austria alone, but the whole house of Europe founded on force went down, for it was founded on sand. Good will is rock, force is sand.

How impossible and weak seems the principle of giving to him that asks! Yet, when we think about it, we realize that while we may disregard these unfortunates we are not able to disregard the effect of them on the whole of life. We are so bound up together that no man can be permanently raised while any man is permanently degraded. I must give to the man something—perhaps not what he asks, but what he needs. I must give him something or else find in the end that something is taken from me. Other-preservation in the end means self-preservation. I do not say this should be the motive, but it is certainly the result. As Booker T. Washington said, "No man can keep another man down in the gutter without staying down with him." This is true economically, socially, politically, and spiritually. And, vice versa, no man can lift another man from the gutter in any of these realms without rising in the process of lifting. In the end the giving "to him that asks" turns out to be rock and selfish withholding turns out to be sand.

When we come to the principle of being inward and secret in our giving, in our praying and in our fasting—how sandlike this seems alongside the immediate returns in the substantial honor we get from letting our giving, our praying, and our renunciations be known! But how quickly all this honor falls to pieces the moment the people begin to suspect that behind these things is the motive of "to be seen of men." It collapses like a house of cards. I once saw a tablet erected by a man who gave a gift to a certain thing, and the titles of the man ran into three lines on the tablet. After reading them all out to a friend I said, "Thou shalt call his name Jesus." The name of the man who proclaimed his greatness in three lines of titles I have forgotten, but I bow at the shrine of this one Name. That one Name is the rock upon which the future civilization of the world will be built —or shattered. In either case it is rock!

To get the best out of two worlds, to lay up on earth and in heaven, to divide your loyalty between God and mammon, to have anxiety for the kingdom of God and for the kingdom of material wants—how sensible and solid that seems! You "diversify" your investments, which is proclaimed as wisdom. But not here, for when this method is put under life we find that it results in inner division, in inner unhappiness, and in final paralysis. The house of man-soul divided against itself cannot stand.

To pick flaws in other people's character, to dispense condemnation—how judicial and wise and solid that seems! And how quickly we seem to go up as others go down. But the market soon collapses. We begin to reap what we sow. Then our attitudes of loveless criticism turn out to be sand.

Should we pursue this further and exhaustively, we would find that everything that Jesus said is founded upon the bedrock of the moral and spiritual facts of the universe. His words are not imposed upon life, but come up out of life. They are life.

I am persuaded that this is the way for which we are made. It is "the kingdom prepared for us from the foundation of the world." Note, "from the foundation of the world"—it is not an after-thought imposed on life, rather it is written in the very constitution of things, in the very make-up of our universe, and of our being.

"The cross is the ground plan of the universe." The Man who announced the Sermon on the Mount had something to do with the make-up of our being, for his words and our beings fit each other. Instead of being foreign laws they are the very laws of our inmost being. When we discover them, we discover the natural way to live. Any other way is like sand in the eye, like acid on a nerve, like hate in the heart—it is corroding, unnatural. The eye was made for light, the ear for music, the heart for love, so our very being was made for Jesus' way of life.

We cannot get away from the challenge and call of Jesus. This witnesses to the fact that his voice awakens within us long-lost chords and we feel that his call is a call to life, real life, our own very life. Jesus said in one place: "My meat is to do the will of him that sent me." The will of God was meat to him, something that fed him instead of poisoning him, something for which his very nature was made. The way of Jesus is my meat, it feeds me, it sustains me, recuperates me, makes me live. Here life catches its rhythm, its harmony, its peace, its song. My mind was made for his thought, my will for his purposes, my emotions for his love. My meat is to his will, but my poison is to do my own will. When I become "worldly-wise" and take my own way, something snaps within me, life grows dull and inane. But when I do his will, I feel universalized; there is a consciousness of at-home-ness in the world, there is a sparkling sense of life. I live and I know it.

One of the very astounding things that Jesus said was: "He that gathereth not with me scattereth." He assumed that those who did not take his way of life would find that the principle of unity within them breaks down; there is a disintegration of personality, the soul forces are scattered by their own centrifugal selfishness. Life will not live unless it lives in the Life. The individual, the group, the nation are held together by the cement of love. Take that out and life breaks down. Christ is that love-cement that keeps life together. The whole of human history is a comment on the verse that he that gathereth not with Jesus scattereth. "Europe has lost Christ, and Europe will perish," said a Russian novelist, and he told the truth, not dogmatically, but out of the burning facts.

At the close of an address on the Sermon on the Mount a Hindu said: "We are all Christians at heart; at least this is the way we feel about it while you are expounding this way of life." He was trying to express what we all feel, namely, that when this way is put before us there is something within us that gives us the sense of this being the soul's homeland, that this is our native air, that we are made for this and for nothing else. Tertullian was right when he said, "The soul is naturally Christian." It is unnaturally something else. Get hold of that truth and it will take the wobble out of Christian living. We will then be Christian with the consent of all our being.

No one can found his life upon this Mind and not feel that he has touched the very ultimate rock. A prominent Hindu said to another Hindu, an Oxford graduate, that a certain Christian was "so very humble."

"Yes," replied the other, "but deep down there is a sense of superiority. Perhaps a better name would be sureness. He feels that he has something of which he is so sure that he can afford to be humble."

He was right. The Christian need not violently assert, for he is inwardly so sure that he can wait—wait until life shall render up its verdict. He knows that he is on rock.

Jesus said that this house of Christian character will be tested from three directions—the "floods" will come from below, the "winds" will blow upon its sides, and the "rain" will descend from above. There is only one side not mentioned—within. But he has been insisting upon inward soundness all the way through his message. Given that inward soundness, he is not afraid to subject this kind of life to the utmost testing from without. He says in effect that nothing from without can break this life; it can be broken only from within.

Luke adds something that is very valuable: When the flood arose, the stream broke against that house and could not shake it: because it was well-builded. Many of us think that putting the foundation of our lives upon the Rock, Christ Jesus, is sufficient. We pay little heed to the kind of a superstructure we build upon him. We do not see that it is "well-builded." The storms and the floods come and we fall under them and wonder why Christ is not more adequate. The Rock is adequate, our superstructure is inadequate. If there has been a crash in religion due to the floods of modern thinking, and the storms of modern stress, then, depend upon it, it is not due to Christ's inadequacy, but due to the crazy structures we have built upon him. Let the foundation be Christ, let the superstructure be Christian, and then let life do its worst or its best. It stands.

But if we lose the Rock, then life does crash about us. Contrast these two: one the philosopher Clifford who lost the Rock, and the other a radiant Christian in our Round Table Conference who had the Rock, but had lost life's most valued physical possession—his eyesight. Clifford says: "I have seen the spring sun shine out of the empty heaven upon a soulless earth, and I have felt with utter loneliness that the Great Companion was dead." Life and its meaning had crashed. But take the Indian Christian: "I have lost my eyesight, but I am not stumbling in darkness. I have light. I am not an old man dreaming dreams, I am a young man seeing visions." Life and its meaning had been subjected to its worst test, but it stood, for it was founded on the Rock and it was well builded.

This philosophy of life which Jesus has given is a *working* philosophy of life. It works. And it works under the most adverse conditions of flood, wind, and rain. It has survival value. In the opening verses Jesus used the word "blessed," which we have found to mean, "happy and deathless." He ends up his message with the same note—the man who founds his life on this way is happy, for he is not dependent upon happenings—he is inwardly determined; and, moreover, he is deathless: "it fell not."

This is victorious vitality.

CHAPTER XVIII

THE AUTHORITY OF JESUS, WANING OR WAXING?

As the crowd listened to Jesus on the hillside the impression he left on them was not that they were listening to an impossible dreamer, or detached mystic, who had no touch with reality. On the contrary they were impressed with his sanity and spiritual authoritativeness. As he talked they felt that the old world they had lived in, built up on greed and selfishness, was the unreal, and that this new world that Jesus was presenting was the only solid reality. "And it came to pass, when Jesus ended these words, the multitudes were astonished at his teachings: for he taught them as one having authority, and not as their scribes" (verses 28, 29).

They felt the difference. The scribes taught rules of religion; Jesus taught "them." A great schoolmaster always insisted that he did not teach Latin, he taught boys. Jesus did not teach principles, he taught persons. Those that heard felt the difference by its warmth and authoritativeness.

Again, the scribes quoted authorities. Jesus spoke out of the authority of living reality. In the words of the scribes they heard the voice of the past; in the words of Jesus they heard the Voice that assumed control over the past, the present, and the future.

The question that forces itself upon us is this: Is this authority of Jesus spent? Is it waxing or waning? Or, as a modern journal puts it, "Is Jesus coming or is he going?" He was able to speak with authority in those simple days, but are these days of complexity and progress too much for him? This age is face to face with Jesus Christ, and the future of religion seems to be bound up with the question of what we are to think of him and his way of life.

Let it be noted first of all that we make too much of the difference between this age of complexity and scientific development and that age of comparative simplicity and traditionalism. Fundamentally, human nature is the same in all ages. The setting of the problems may change but the problems are really the same: selfishness, contempt for others, lack of faith in the healing power of love, divided personality, unreality, the dominance of the material, the need of a moral cleansing, a dynamic, God—these are as fresh to-day as when he dealt with them on the mountainside. Moreover, there is one important fact that must be noted, namely, that he provides for the change in the setting of the problem by allowing for development. His method of dealing with the old, "Ye have heard it said of old time, . . . but I say unto you," shows that he was not traditional, but experimental in his attitudes. His other sayings, such as "I have yet many things to say unto you, but ye cannot bear them now"; and, "when he, the Spirit of truth, is come, he shall guide you into all truth," open the gates for progressive revelation even while speaking in terms that have the air of finality upon them.

But the question persists, Is Jesus coming or is he going? I know the questioning of his final authority, even within the ranks of those who follow him. The undertone of fear is that he was Eastern and simple and unable to grapple with the complexities of this age, especially with life in the West.

In answer let us take a case in which the problems of East and West, ancient and modern, center. The modern scientific dominant West meets the awakening East in India. Every single problem of modern days seems to center in this one problem of the relationship between Britain and India. As Lord Irwin and Mahatma Gandhi sat face to face, almost every single modern problem—economic, social, political, racial, personal—was focused there, at least in germ. Out of the seemingly hopeless tangle they found a way—at any rate the first steps—to the way out. How did they do it? The representatives of the newspapers asked Mahatma Gandhi, "What miracle turned the tide of negotiations when everything seemed lost?" His answer was,

"Goodness on the part of Lord Irwin; and if I may say so, apologetically, goodness on my own part. Then it was the application of the principles of the Sermon on the Mount that brought peace." In this complex situation was Jesus authoritative? To that situation apply force, apply unbending self-assertion, apply anything except the way of Jesus, and it would have ended in a breakdown and an impasse. A touch of the mind of Jesus and closed doors open. I am persuaded that there is not a single modern problem that could not be solved if we approached it in his spirit.

I am not sufficiently in touch with the West to interpret it, but I can say of the East that Christ is rising to moral and spiritual dominance. There are cross-currents it is true, and there are oppositions, but nevertheless out of the strife and clash of ideals he is rising dominant. Call the roll of the reforms that are taking place in the East to-day, whether in the social, economic, political, or religious life, and you will find that every single reform—if it be a reform and not a reaction—is going straight toward Christ. Not one is going away from him. Wherever the situation is moving on to the better he is ruling the development. A Hindu chairman—and he was not at all friendly—put it this way: "We have to face the status of women, of the depressed classes, and our problems in general in the light of what the Christians teach." You could feel that the Light that was lighting the way was the mind of Christ.

Another prominent Hindu high up in official life said, before a large audience: "The Spirit of Christ is the thing that is going to bring together East and West. If you took a plebiscite of the educated classes, you would find Christ occupying a very high place in the minds of educated Indians. We may not be outwardly Christians but we are more and more becoming Christian in spirit."

As we walked away from a meeting in which I had been fiercely cross-questioned by the Hindus and Moslems, a very thoughtful Hindu, a college professor, said, "Whatever they may say, it is a fact nevertheless that ninety per cent of the world's best thought is revolving about Jesus Christ."

A Hindu teacher in a high school put the matter to me in this way: "I firmly believe that the example and ideal set forth by the Lord Jesus Christ in his life is the ideal toward which the world is slowly but surely progressing. History points to it. And I am sure the time will come, after how much time I cannot say, when the world will be a Christian world, not in the external dogmatic sense—that is of going to church and being baptized—but in the real sense of following and living up to the ideal which the Lord Jesus exemplified to perfection in his life."

Men may stay in their old forms, but Christ has hold of them. The headmaster of a high school said to his students in my presence, "I am a Brahman of the Brahmans, a member of the most bigoted sect of India, and yet I say to you students that I have been moved to the depths this week. I cannot say I want to be a Christian, but I do want to be Christlike."

Said a Hindu to a Scotch vice-chancellor of a university, "Yes, India will become Christian, but she will never call herself Christian." One can see the reason for that statement, while he cannot be satisfied with it, for there is a clash going on between East and West and the East feels that she cannot afford to adopt the religion of her conquerors. That would make her lose her own national soul. But she cannot escape the One who is the heart of that religion. "Christ is the one hope of our country," said a Hindu law member to a friend of mine.

"Then why don't you follow him?" my friend asked.

"You do not understand that we live two lives—one outside and one inside our homes. For fear of our homes we remain as we are," was the reply.

Men may repudiate the West (while at the very moment of repudiation they are often taking from it!), they may repudiate the system we have built up around Christ, but Christ is gripping men everywhere. In one of our Round Table

Conferences a beautiful-spirited inspector of schools said in a most moving way: "I was isolated as a member of the so-called low castes and I turned to Christ as the one who died on the cross for all. But when I turned to Christianity I was dumbfounded. It was not like him. I therefore decided to extract Christ from Christianity and take him. So I follow him." There were tears in our hearts as we listened to these sincere words—tears of sorrow that our Christianity was not like him; and yet there were tears of joy that, in spite of the imperfections of the system called by his name, the perfect Christ was holding men. I do not see anything else that is holding men. A young professor said to a group of us in a Round Table Conference: "Everything is gone—everything except the character of Christ. I hold to that. But it is all I have." And that was enough. With that Key in his hand he could unlock the door to God, to life. But lose that Key and God and life are unsolved enigmas.

Can we get away from him? We cannot—and live. Two examples come to my mind, of two men who tried to get away from him and found themselves face to face with him. One was a European, who became disgusted with the artificiality of modern life, threw off the trappings of Western civilization, and became to all intents and purposes a Hindu Sannyasi. I met him seated on the bank of a river in one of the holy places of India and said to him, "Now tell me what is the result of your becoming a Sannyasi—what have you found?"

He thoughtfully replied, "The sum total of my becoming a Sannyasi is that I have been drawn nearer to Jesus Christ."

There in that quietness, with everything stripped away from him, he found himself face to face with the inescapable Christ.

The other one was an able Brahman professor, who became a Christian and then, finding himself not at home in the Christian Church, was taken back into Hinduism with a great deal of ceremony and rejoicing on the part of the Hindus. "There, Christ has failed," they said. Had he? After being back in Hinduism for several years this professor was in one of our Round Table Conferences. This is what he said, "I am still not free. I have not yet found peace. I put on these outward symbols to hide my inner feelings. I owe a great deal to Christianity." Later, when I heard him speak I saw that the "one dear Face" was haunting, moving him and that he was saying within himself, "Lord, to whom else can we go? thou hast the words of eternal life." Physically, can we run away from gravity? Emotionally, can we run away from love? If so, then spiritually we can run away from Christ.

A prominent Hindu in a Round Table Conference said: "You have given us four days of heaven on earth. It would be a good thing if there were one religion so that all strife might cease. It may be that Christ is that religion. We must put out the cradle to receive the Christ-child into our hearts so that he may grow up in us." In the early days there was no room for him in the Inn. Here in India there has been the Great Hesitation. But India is discovering more and more what we are all discovering—that without him the house of man-soul is empty. They are putting out the cradle.

Four years have gone by since I published *Christ at the Round Table*. Have I been compelled to alter the conclusions I recorded there, namely, that by actual experimentation Christ is proving the Way? After four years more of Round Tables I have no alteration to make except in the way of added emphasis. As I have listened in to the finest that the religious East could produce I have been struck with the fact that outside of Christ men were uncertain, fumbling. In Christ they had found God or, rather, God had found them. And with it they had found a working way to live. They were rejoicing. One Moslem lawyer, surprised at this, said at the close of one of these Conferences: "I have come to the conclusion that the Christians were not as frank and honest as the non-Christians, for all of you Christians said you had found something, while we Hindus and Moslems all said we had found nothing. Therefore you must have lacked our frankness." I quietly suggested that there was another alternative: Christ is the Way!

He stands blocking the forces of secularism and irreligion in East and West. He is taking the brunt of the attack upon religion. A young man of deep earnestness and brilliance, after asking me questions for hours before an audience, finally said: "I am not against Christianity as such. I am against all religion. I want to wipe it all out. But men like you are our difficulty." I told him that I was not his difficulty, but that the Christ whom I presented was the real difficulty in getting rid of religion. I told him he could knock to pieces by fierce invective the dogmatisms, the superstitions, and the anti-human attitudes of religion, but that when he faced Christ, religion met him not as dogmatism, not as superstition, not as anti-human, but as supreme sanity, as open-mindedness, as self-giving love, as a moral and spiritual renovation, as a moral ideal compellingly final, as life itself.

"But," you ask, "isn't there a revival of the old faiths in the East?" Yes, seemingly so. But along with this revival there is constant, inner, steady decay. Moreover, the great part of this revival is the result of the Spirit of Christ galvanizing the old into activity. He challenges faiths as well as persons. I once saw the sun rising in the West. At least I thought I did! There it was, a huge golden disk! But I soon realized that it was the setting moon and that its golden hue was the reflected light of the rising sun. Many systems that now seem to take on the luster of rising life are soon found to have only the reflected light of the ascending Christ. They are not rising suns, they are setting moons—illuminated just before they set. All religions that have passed away have been revived just before the passing. Light flared up —and went out, exhausted.

I see no signs that the hold of Jesus upon the human heart is weakening. On the contrary, he is becoming more and more authoritative. He is becoming more and more authoritative because he does not impose laws on life. He expounds life itself, and he regenerates it. A very thoughtful and evidently perplexed Hindu said, "This that you present makes religion possible for those of us who have come in contact with modern life and thought." It does. For, as one great thinker has said, "There is nothing in the teachings of Christ which the subsequent growth of human knowledge will render obsolete." I cannot say this of any other. A Hindu, at the close of a series of meetings, said: "He is growing. Each time he comes he seems to have a greater message. We hope, therefore, that the next time he comes he will speak in the same terms of Buddha and Krishna as he now does of Christ." But how could I? I respect and even love Buddha (I wish I could say the same of

Krishna, but, alas, I cannot), but I see no one whom I can put in the same category with Christ. I expect to grow, and I expect my message to grow—for are we not following the unfolding Christ?—but beyond the sublimity, the power, the moral excellence, the saving glory of this Man the human mind will not progress. Said Rodin, the great sculptor, "Beyond Phidias art does not progress." Beyond Christ religion or moral progress does not go. Beyond Christ? If this Sermon on the Mount is his mind, then this is a mount for humanity to scale in the future and not a foothill which humanity has explored and transcended. Transcended? The only objection we can bring against Christ is that his life is too lofty, and too grand, and his mind too demanding of us. Our very objection proves that he is ahead of us and not behind us.

I was in the birthplace of a modern Messiah, who was to incarnate and hence transcend the Christ of the Gospels. The students of the college of which he is the patron said to him on his return from Europe, "Now, please don't talk to us about your Messiahship, but tell us something of your travels in Europe." I cannot imagine people asking Jesus about his travels. You may hate him and reject him, but you cannot help seeing in him a supreme moral issue. As Professor Ellwood says, "The greatest problem of the future development of religion upon this planet is what shall be done with Jesus and his teachings. . . . We cannot get away from Christ in religion any more than we can get away from Copernicus in astronomy and still remain sound and sane."

After one of our Round Tables a cultured Moslem said: "One thing that struck me very forcibly in this group was the fact that while the rest of us were uncertain, all of you Christians to a man seemed to hold a passionate loyalty to Christ. I regret this." I do not! For that loyalty has meant life. Amid the clash of things he holds us. And that holding is the most precious and saving thing in life. If he goes, then our universe crashes about us.

An Englishman, high up in government authority in India, said at the close of an address, "I see no way out of our present difficulties, except as we Englishmen and you Indians both catch the spirit of Christ and live it out in our relationships with each other." A Hindu nationalist arose and said, "This lifts a cloud from our horizon, for if our problems are faced in the spirit of Christ, then a solution will be found." I know of no problem in East or West which, if faced in the spirit of Jesus, would not be settled in one of two ways: we would either solve that problem, or, if we failed to solve it, we would grow taller and finer in the process of an attempted solution. We might fail, but it would be the failure of Calvary, which was the world's greatest failure and the world's greatest success.

In the book of Revelation Jesus says, "I am the Alpha and the Omega"—the first and the last letters of the Greek alphabet. In other words, he is the Christ of the Beginnings and the Christ of the Final Word. The Christ of the Beginnings! Yes, and how amazingly he began! He spoke these great words on the mount and lived them, every one—and more. In the Sermon he taught men to pray, "Our Father, . . . forgive us our trespasses," but he himself never prayed that prayer. He said to those about him, "If you, then, being evil," and then quietly left himself out of that category. He made "for righteousness' sake" and "for my sake" the same, identifying himself with the very righteousness of the universe. He implied that the phrases, "I never knew you," and not doing "the will of the Father," were identical and meant the same thing. High words? Yes, but there was nothing but harmony between those high words and his own high life. The scrutinizing, sifting centuries have seen no reason to alter what he said either about himself or about life.

He is the Christ of the Final Word.

The Sermon on the Mount is the transcript of his mind and spirit. Said a leading Hindu official after an address on the Sermon on the Mount, "If this is Christianity that the speaker is expounding, then it commands our reverence and respect." Yes, it does command our reverence and respect, but more—it commands our obedience, and our very all.

It is a working philosophy of life—the only one that will work. For the universe backs this way of life.